EMBELLISH ME

First published in the United States by

Interweave Press LLC
201 East Fourth Street
Loveland, CO 80537
www.interweave.com

Copyright © RotoVision SA 2012

Library of Congress Cataloging-in-Publication Data
Wisbrun, Laurie.
Embellish me : how to print, dye, and decorate your fabric / Laurie Wisbrun.
pages cm
Includes bibliographical references and index.
ISBN 978-1-59668-862-9 (flexibound)
1. Textile crafts. 2. Textile printing. 3. Dyes and dyeing--Textile fibers. I. Title.TT699.
W57 2012
667.38--dc23
2011052806

Layout: Alphabetical
Art director: Emily Portnoi
Art editor: Jennifer Osborne
Cover design: Julia Boyles
Cover photo: Ryann Ford, ryannford.com
Photo styling: Robin Finlay
Commissioning editor: Isheeta Mustafi

EMBELLISH ME

How to Print, Dye, and Decorate Your Fabric

Laurie Wisbrun

INTERWEAVE
interweave.com

 PART 1
The Basics

② **PART 2**
Techniques

 PART 3
Going Pro

 PART 4
Resources

INTRODUCTION

by Laurie Wisbrun

As you start to ponder the types of fabric you can alter, and all the goodies you can embellish, you'll begin to recognize the possibilities as endless. I remember as a little girl, when I discovered paint pens, I took to personalizing everything I could get my hands on. As I ran out of fabric items to customize in my wardrobe and bedroom (handpainted shoes, jackets, and book bags were some of my favorites!), I started personalizing our household appliances. Handmade fabric tags covered with glitter and paint pen swirls suddenly began to appear on everything in our house . . . plants, washing machine, refrigerator, dining table, the dog . . . Nothing was off limits.

In the past, I thought the word "embellished" was somehow synonymous with "gaudy" and it brought to mind mounds of rhinestones and the bedazzled items of the 1970s. But as I've gotten older and become more confident in my artistic voice, embellishment has turned into a way of making something more special and unique.

I love that, due to the nature of hand-decorated items, each piece is one of a kind. We've all been in the midst of a project when you have the moment where you're convinced that with that one slip of the hand, you've just managed to destroy your creation. Those "aarrgh, oh no!" parts of a project where the pattern you envisioned in your head doesn't look much like what you ended up drawing with your pen. Or when you didn't quite get enough ink on the stamp and the coverage isn't quite as even as you had intended. But at the end of most of my projects I find—more often than not—that those little portions end up being my favorite elements of what I created. So, my advice to you is to celebrate the inconsistencies and little imperfections in what you create. Don't try to make it perfect. It can take all the fun out of the experimentation and the impromptu nature of creating something all your own.

When I set out to write this book, I knew I wanted to develop a reference guide that featured an extensive number of approaches to embellishing. I wanted it to feature sophisticated and artistic approaches. With that in mind, I had my heart set on collaborating with some of my favorite artists so each of them could demonstrate their own unique spin on their featured techniques.

Each tutorial in this book will equip you with the information you need to experiment with the technique, leaving you with the freedom to apply the approach in your own way. Galleries and interviews with the chapter contributors feature beautiful examples of embellished items to further inspire your own creative vision. In the final chapter you'll find interviews with cutting-edge artists who have taken embellishment to completely new levels and who have been gracious enough to share their insights into how they maintain inspiration, create collections, and market their artistic work.

I have loved creating this book and I hope it becomes a treasured new resource and a source of inspiration for you.

Zippered pouch by Laurie Wisbrun. Features hand-dyed fabric with bleach-resist bird motif and machine-drawn embroidery. Appliqué and pieced portions incorporate hand screen-printed Hearts fabric by Umbrella Prints.

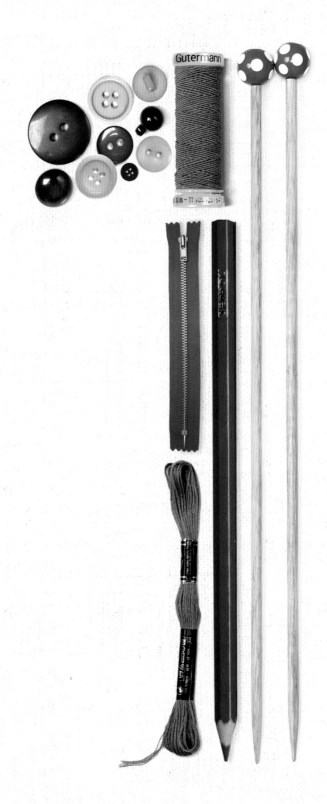

1 GETTING STARTED

by Laurie Wisbrun

Part of exploring embellishing is arming yourself with an array of tools and materials to allow you to experiment with different techniques. This chapter touches on some of the basic items you should have on hand, but don't limit your toolkit to just these items. It can be extremely satisfying to open your craft bins or drawers and find the perfect item to incorporate into your latest project, or that tool you were never sure if you would use. All those bits, bobs, and craft weapons you've been collecting are about to be put to great use.

TOOLS AND MATERIALS

Depending on what type of embellishing you plan to do, you may need a variety of tools and materials. These lists cover some of the goodies to keep in your toolkit.

General

- Pens, pencils, and sketch paper
- Tracing paper
- Graph paper
- Lightweight sheets of cardboard
- Adhesives (glue sticks, sprays, glue gun, jewelry epoxy)
- Ribbons, buttons, lace, and varied trims
- Zippers and fringe
- Trinkets and charms
- Beading needles (very fine in order to work with tiny bead holes)
- Beads of different sizes
- Paper ephemera (originally used to describe vintage paper but the rise in scrapbooking has led to a surge in reproduction paper items that have a vintage feel)

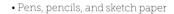

Cyanotype printing

- Ink-jet transparency film

- Cyanotype kit (with bottles)

- Soda ash (sodium carbonate)

- Tannic acid

- Sodium alginate thickener

- Dye-resist paste

- Hydrogen peroxide

- Picture frame (glass and backing)

- Plastic squeeze bottles

- Gloves

- Measuring cups and spoons

- Foam brush

- Plastic clips

Dyeing, bleaching, and painting

- Safety materials (gloves, goggles, mask, and dye box)

- Fabric dyes and paints (check manufacturer descriptions for the type best suited to the surface you're working on and the technique you're using)

- Permanent fabric pens, pencils, and chalks

- Salt (helps the fabric to absorb the dye, which helps create deeper colors)

- Urea (a moisture-drawing agent that keeps the fabric damper for longer during the dyeing process, resulting in deeper, brighter colors)

- Soda ash (a dye activator that fixes reactive dyes so they are permanent and do not wash out)

- Household bleach

- Bleach pen

- Anti-Chlor Neutralizer (stops the bleaching action of bleach)

- Stainless steel or enamel dye pot

- Natural dyestuff

- Alum and cream of tartar mordant (to prepare fabric for natural dyes)

- Non-corrosive pipe sections and string (for shibori)

- Soy wax

- Measuring spoons

- Non-corrosive stirring tools

- A variety of plastic containers

- Plastic squeeze bottles

- Mixing cups

- Natural bristle and sponge brushes

- Textile detergent (a pre- and post-wash detergent specially formulated for dyed fabric to reduce washout and fading)

- Iron and ironing board

TOOLS AND MATERIALS

Sewing

- Different sizes of needles
- Straight pins
- Safety pins (curved pins are great for quilting projects)
- Colored threads
- Thread nippers
- Fabric
- Fabric interfacing (used to stiffen fabric or give it some weight; different weights are available)
- Water-soluble pens, pencils, and tailor's chalk (for adding temporary marks on fabric)
- Sewing machine
- Iron and ironing board

Cutting

- Paper scissors
- Fabric scissors (don't cut anything other than fabric with these as it will dull the blades)
- Pinking shears (scissors with a sawtooth edge; prevents fabric edges from fraying when cut)
- Cutting mat
- Rotary cutter (different blades are available for different cuts)
- Cutting rulers
- Small hobby knife for precise cutting and making stencils)
- Craft knife

Appliqué, embroidery, and punchneedle

- Embroidery hoops
- Embroidery floss and yarns
- Beeswax thread conditioner
  (to help work with coarse threads,
  like metallic floss)
- Fabric stabilizer (stiffens fabric
  and keeps your appliqué piece from
  moving around while you're working)
- Fusible webbing (to attach an
  appliqué piece without sewing)
- Tapestry and embroidery needles
- Needlepunch tool and wire
- Needle threader
- Embroidery scissors
- Transfer paper
- Spray bottle
- Water soluble pens
  (for marking fabric)
- Aida cloth (an open weave fabric
  with a mesh suited for cross-stitch)

Printing, stamping, and stenciling

- Pencils and black markers
- Acetate film
- Fabric screen-printing ink
- Squeegee
- Silk screen
- Butter knife or spatula
- Masking tape/sticky tape
- Felt underlay
- Ink roller
- Glass or plastic mat
- Lino carving tools
- Easy-to-carve print block
  (or wood or linoleum block)
- White office paper
- Fabric wax crayons, markers, and pens
- Iron
- Iron-on transfer paper printed with
  image or design from an ink-jet printer
  (see manufacturer's instructions)

UNDERSTANDING FABRIC

Fiber types

Before you start a new project, it's important to consider what type of fabric or fiber you'll be using. Some textiles are better suited to some techniques than others. If you're purchasing new fabric specifically for a project, check the label to find out what type of material it is. But in some cases, especially if you're working with a new pre-made, finished good (like a book bag) or vintage treasure, you may not be able to definitively determine the type of fabric. If you can, experiment on a small piece before you dive in.

All fabric is made from two types of fiber. Synthetic fibers are man-made and natural fibers are derived from sources including plants such as flax or bamboo, or animals such as silkworms or sheep. Examples of natural fibers include wool, cotton, linen, and silk; synthetic fibers include polyester, nylon, and rayon. There are also blended fabrics that contain more than one type of fabric. This can be a blend of both synthetic and natural fibers (nylon/wool) or a blend within the same category of fiber (linen/cotton).

Understanding fiber type is especially important if you'll be using dyes or inks as they can react with fabric differently than how you might expect. Fabrics will take dyes and inks differently, so your colors may not be as bright or saturated as you would hope, or they may shift in color. When working with dyes and inks, first read the product instructions to see what's recommended.

If you're buying fabric yardage to dye, a good bet is to look for PFD (prepared for dyeing) fabrics. PFD fabric is unbleached, has an off-white color, and will take dyes better than non-PFD fabrics. In order for fabric to be white it is bleached, washed, and then sometimes treated with a whitening agent or with sizing. You can dye fabrics that are not PFD, but they may not take the color as well.

Categories of fabric

A trip to any fabric store is a quick reminder of just how many different types of fabric are manufactured. The following pages provide an overview of several common categories.

Felt—a non-woven fabric that's made by matting and condensing the fibers into a fabric with a woolen texture. As with all fabrics, there are many different grades (and prices). Some felts are pure wool, some are a blend of synthetic and natural fibers, and others are 100-percent synthetic (least expensive and often labeled as Craft Felt). Because the edges of felt won't fray when cut, it is a great option to choose for appliqué.

Linen—made from the fiber of the flax plant, linens are smooth to the touch and have a light, airy quality that make them an ideal option for clothing. When used in home décor and accessories, linen can convey a sense of richness or elegance. When a fabric (even when made of cotton or other non-flax fibers) is woven in a texture that is similar to linen, it may be labeled as a linen weave.

Cotton—made from the seedpod of the cotton plant, cottons are a natural fiber fabric.

Cottons and cotton blends are the most widely used fabric in the manufacture of clothing, so if you're embellishing a pre-made piece of apparel, there's a good chance that it's made from cotton. Cotton takes dye easily and is easy to work with due to its soft hand. Most printed quilting fabrics are made from cotton.

Different cotton weaves produce different types of fabric. Gingham, percale, chambray, and broadcloth are all plain weaves. Denim, cotton duck, and gabardines are all twill weave fabrics and are more durable. They are popular options in home décor fabrics. Sateens are satin weave and have a higher sheen.

Knits—a fabric made of rows of loops called stitches, which are connected in rows. From casual sweatshirt fleece to more elegant knit velvets, knits are easy to sew with and are a popular option for apparel.

Burlap—a fabric made from hemp fiber. Although the texture of burlap is not soft, it's a great option for projects like bags or storage boxes and can be an interesting fabric choice for stamping or screen printing.

Silk—a natural protein fiber made from the cocoon of silk worms. Manufacturing silk requires a great deal of handling and processing, so it is also one of the most expensive types of fabric. Silk fibers have a radiance and shimmer, which makes them a beautiful option for a wide range of projects. Silks take dye beautifully.

Understanding fabric grain

All knit and woven fabric has a grain, which means that the threads run in two different directions (vertical and horizontal). Grain affects how a fabric will stretch and drape, so if you're going to create garments with your fabric, it's important to identify the grain before you start to cut your fabric.

Woven fabrics—fibers run at a 90-degree angle to each other. The weave can be loose or tight and may have some give in it, but will only stretch on the bias. Cutting a fabric on the bias will result in a garment draping differently than one cut on the crosswise grain.

Lengthwise grain—runs parallel to the fabric selvedges and has no stretch.

Crosswise grain—runs perpendicular to the fabric selvedges and has a slight stretch.

Bias—runs at a 45-degree angle to the fabric selvedge and has lots of stretch.

Knit fabrics—a knit can stretch in one or both directions and is made from loops of fiber that allow it to be stretchy. The grain for knit fabrics is defined in the same way for knits as it is for woven ones.

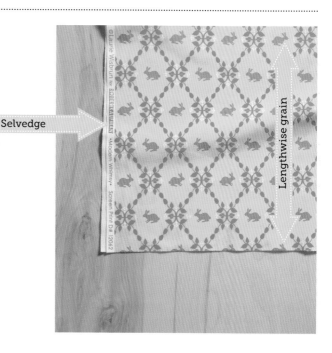

2 DESIGNING PATTERNS

by Heather Dutton

Simply put, a pattern is a repeating motif artfully put together to create an overall decorative design. It sounds pretty basic, but the role that pattern plays in our daily lives is anything but simple. The use of pattern helps create a sense of individuality, adds character to our homes, and enhances our overall visual experience. It's no wonder that the art of embellishing surfaces has been around for centuries.

We're surrounded by the beauty of pattern everywhere we look. It's on the clothing we wear, the dishes we use, even the shopping bags we carry to the market. Whether it's abstract, representational, whimsical or sophisticated, pattern has the ability to transform an object from mundane to memorable.

Simply looking at a pattern can transport you to a different era. It can evoke a mood and even suggest a gender. The power of pattern is remarkable when you think about it.

Creating a successful pattern design begins with a well thought out motif, but the decisions you make regarding color, scale, and composition are equally important. Each decision plays a key role in the design process and can help to shape the overall visual impact of your design.

Whether you're designing a pattern for embroidery, block printing, appliqué, beading, or screen-printing, it's easy to feel overwhelmed by the number of decisions that need to be made. In this chapter I'll walk you through some of the general principles of pattern design to help you better understand the decision-making process and how your choices affect your finished pattern. You'll learn how the different types of motifs are categorized, as well as the important roles that color, scale, and composition play in the design process.

Also included in the chapter are two tutorials demonstrating how to create your own pattern repeat—by hand and digitally. Armed with this knowledge and a few basic skills you'll be on your way to creating your own repeat pattern before you know it!

GENERAL PATTERN DESIGN TIPS

Understanding the general principles of pattern design and finding the creative process that works best for you is the key to creating a successful pattern. To help you get started on your creative journey, here are some elements you should consider when planning your design.

Pattern categories

Patterns are used in a wide variety of markets and can include countless types of motifs. To help organize the vast array of patterns, the surface design industry has created a set of categories based on the primary motif in the design. Although not exclusive, the following categories are the industry standard.

Conversational or novelty pattern—

a design where the primary motif is a recognizable object, animal, or character. Holiday-themed designs such as Christmas trees, snowflakes, pumpkins, or hearts also fall into this category. Conversational patterns have a tendency to be whimsical, but a sophisticated butterfly design would still be considered a conversational pattern because of the motif.

Conversational pattern. Rainy London Clouds by Amy King.

Floral pattern. Succulents by Oksancia–Oksana Pasishnychenko.

Floral pattern—not only includes floral motifs, but also other plant life, such as leaves, vines, or seedpods. For example, a botanical or tropical design featuring natural elements would be placed into the floral category.

Geometric pattern or geo—a design where the primary motif is either a traditional or abstracted geometric shape. The motifs can include circles, squares, diamonds, or facets. Geometric designs typically have a strong graphic appeal, whether the layout is regimented or organic simply because of the nature of the motif itself. Stripes, dots, or plaids also fall under this category.

Ethnic pattern—typically based on folk art-inspired motifs, cultural elements, or techniques from around the globe. These can include motifs like Turkish tiles, Aztec designs, mosaics, or paisleys, for example. They can also represent techniques such as batik, embroidery, weaving, or block printing.

Textures—a unique category of pattern design because the primary element is typically abstract. It can include things such as brush strokes, paint spatter, cross hatch, or wood grain. Animal skins and camouflage also fit within the textures category.

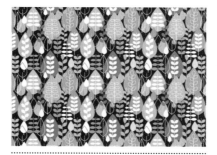
Floral pattern. Mod Leaves by Alison Tauber.

Ethnic pattern. Tribal by Lydia Meiying.

Geometric pattern. Navy Ikat by Andrea Whalen.

Texture. Fuzzy Zebra—Light by Andrea M. Wolf.

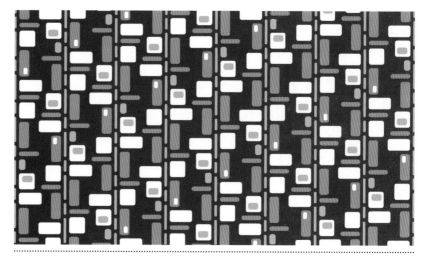
Geometric pattern. Blocked by Zesti-Ine Beerten.

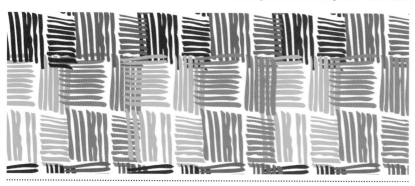
Texture. Line Play by Cheryl Warrick.

Texture. Textured Color by Jim Keaton.

Umbraline Block (in pink and in magenta) by Holli Zollinger.

Color

Color is a powerful tool in all forms of art and plays a particularly strong role in shaping the overall aesthetic of your pattern. The simple use of color can set the tone of your design, making your pattern feel whimsical or sophisticated. It can also evoke a particular season or suggest a gender. The decisions you make regarding color and its placement within your design can dramatically alter the look of your pattern.

Something as simple as changing the background color from light to dark can affect how the pattern reads and change the visual relationship between the elements. You can add movement by using multiple colors, or you can create a rich, subtle effect by using tonal shades of a single color. This technique is referred to as tone on tone. A tone on tone pattern can appear to be solid from a distance, but the motifs become more visible the closer you look. Tone on tone patterns are commonly used on quilting fabrics or in damask designs. Don't be afraid to experiment and play around with multiple color options while you're working on your pattern. Sometimes you can discover an unexpected quality that's hidden within your design simply by changing the color placement.

Butterfly Damask by Patty Sloniger.

Delicious Damask Pink
by Shannon Benavidez of Mayabella Creations.

Lime Mojito Damask by Cynthia K. Strickland.

Mod Grain Blue by Lori Kishlar and
Sarah Melancon.

Large-scale pattern. Peony decorative pillow cover by Whitlock & Co.

Large-scale pattern. Pillow cover, handmade by Emilia Priscila.

Large-scale pattern. Chartreuse Twirly pillow cover, handmade by Tara Stewart. Fabric by Premier Prints.

Scale

Scale is another important aspect to consider when planning your pattern. The proportion of your motif, and how it relates to the other elements within the design, can dramatically alter the overall mood and set the tone for your pattern. Changing the scale of the design can make it feel contemporary, sweet, graphic, or sophisticated. It's also important to consider how the scale of your pattern relates to your finished product. The surface design industry has defined the most dramatic uses of scale with the following two categories:

Large-scale—an allover pattern where the motif is dramatically oversized, creating a bold visual statement. This typically gives the pattern a contemporary feel and is commonly used on home furnishings and décor.

Ditsy—an allover pattern where the motifs are very small and typically have a compact layout. This creates a sweet, diminutive effect and is often used to complement a primary design within a pattern collection.

Repeat and composition

Another key decision is the composition and repeat layout. Consider whether or not you want your pattern to feel airy, compact, organic, or regimented. These choices will help you select the best repeat layout to visually express your design. The three most commonly used repeat layouts include tile, half drop, and brick. A tile repeat creates an even, linear design, a half-drop repeat creates a diagonal effect, and a brick repeat creates a horizontally staggered layout (see pages 28–31 for more information).

Once you've familiarized yourself with these general principles—and how they affect your design—you'll open up a world of possibilities for creating compelling patterns. Let your creativity run wild, don't be afraid to experiment, and, most importantly, have fun!

Ditsy pattern. Reproduction feed sack necktie by Brianna Venner.

Ditsy pattern. Liberty of London neckties by Jane Johnson / Tux and Tulle. Fabric by Liberty of London.

HAND-RENDERED PATTERNS

1   Starting with a blank piece of paper, begin sketching out your design in the center of the page. It's important to keep your drawing away from all the outer edges of the paper for this part of the process. I like to start my drawing in pencil in case I decide to make changes along the way. If you prefer, you can always go back over the design in pen once you're happy with it.

2   Turn your paper over and divide it in half both vertically and horizontally using a pencil. Mark these lines lightly so they don't show through on the other side of the paper. When you're done, you should have four equal squares on your page. Using the numbers 1–4, write one number in each square of your grid as shown.

TOOLS AND MATERIALS
- Paper
- Pencil/pen
- Eraser
- Ruler
- Paper scissors
- Colored pencils or markers
- Tape
- Scanner

1

Hints and tips

Creating a hand-rendered pattern is not only fun, it's also a simple way to learn the basics of how a repeat is physically put together.

When you're selecting your paper, keep in mind that your paper size will be the size of your pattern repeat. If you want to design a small or large repeat, your paper size needs to reflect that. It's also helpful to choose a paper size that's easily divisible by two, so you don't have to do a lot of math in order to divide your paper in half.

3 This next part might be hard to swallow, but you're going to take your scissors and cut your drawing in half vertically. Scary, I know! Since you've worked hard on your design so far, it's a great idea to either scan or photocopy your drawing before cutting so that you have a copy of the original.

4 Reverse the horizontal placement of the two cut pieces so your drawings are now positioned on the outer left and right edges of the paper. The number grid on the back of your paper should now read 2, 1, 4, 3, as shown.

5 Tape the two pieces back together again in their new position. Place the tape on the back of the paper so it doesn't interfere with your drawing and try to match the seams as closely as possible. The seam should barely be visible once you've finished taping your pieces together.

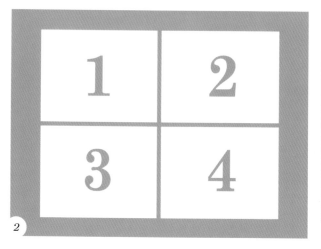

2

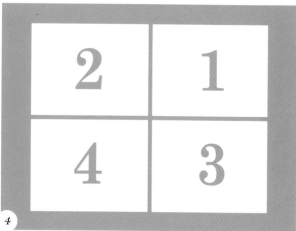

4

3

5

6   Cut your drawing in half again, this time cutting across the paper horizontally.

7   Reverse the vertical placement of the two cut pieces so your drawings are now positioned at the top and bottom edges. The number grid on the back of your paper should now read 4, 3, 2, 1.

8   Tape the two pieces back together again in their new position, remembering to place the tape on the backside of your paper. The paper should now have drawings in all four outer corners, leaving the center of the page empty.

9   Fill in the rest of the empty space with your design. If you have motifs that need to be placed on the edges of the paper in order to get a balanced design, simply turn your drawing over and gently roll the two edges of the paper together so they're touching. Gently press the paper down, keeping the edges together, and draw your motif so it crosses both sides of the paper. When you turn your drawing back over, you'll see that you've successfully filled in the space on both sides of the paper.

6

8

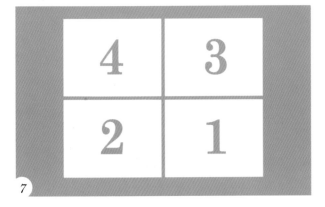

7

9

Hints and tips

If you're designing a linear geometric pattern, use your ruler to line up the placement of your new motifs with your originals. This will ensure that your finished repeat has the precision that is usually seen in linear geometric designs.

Before uploading your scanned repeat to a digital fabric printer, double-check your digital file and make any small edits that might be necessary to ensure your repeat is perfectly seamless.

10 Congratulations! You've now created a repeatable tile design!

11 Adding color is a nice way to finish off your design. Color can be applied either by hand or digitally. If you're coloring your pattern by hand, it's a good idea to either scan or photocopy your finished drawing so you have a copy of the final repeat before adding color. This comes in handy if you want to try different variations.

12 Now that your repeat pattern is complete, it can be uploaded to a digital fabric printer (such as spoonflower.com) or you can use it as a template for your next block printing, appliqué, embroidery, or screen-printing project.

10

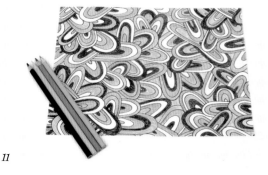

11

12

COMPUTER-RENDERED PATTERNS

Tile repeat

1 Begin by creating a new document. I've chosen a canvas size of 900 pixels x 900 pixels (3" x 3") with a resolution of 300 pixels per inch. You'll need to know these dimensions in pixels further into the tutorial, so it's a good idea to jot them down now. Select your color mode, choose White from the Background Contents menu, and select OK.

Your canvas size will be the size of your finished repeat, so keep this in mind when choosing your dimensions. It's best to select dimensions that are easily divisible by two.

2 Create a new layer, name it Motif, and either paste in a previously scanned drawing or create a new drawing using Photoshop's drawing tools. Place your drawing in the center of your canvas, making sure none of the elements are touching the outer edges.

Photoshop's Snap feature and Guides are both useful tools to help center your design and line up new elements that you create.

3 Photoshop's Offset Filter easily replicates the cut and paste method you learned earlier in the hand-rendered pattern tutorial. With your Motif layer selected, choose Filter, Other, and Offset from the top menu.

4 To calculate the offset dimensions for a tile repeat, divide your original dimensions in half. For example, if your original canvas was 900 pixels x 900 pixels, input Horizontal 450 pixels and Vertical 450 pixels. Choose Wrap Around in the Undefined Areas and select OK. Your drawing should now be placed in all four corners, leaving the center of your canvas empty.

TOOLS AND MATERIALS
- Adobe Photoshop
- Digital image of your design

Hints and tips

Include the dimension of your repeat tile when naming your pattern swatch in case you want to create multiple size options for the same design.

5 To create a balanced layout, fill any open gaps in your repeat, making sure not to move the existing elements of your design.

6 Congratulations! You've successfully created a digital tile repeat. To add color to your design, create a new layer underneath your Motif layer, name it Color, and use any of Photoshop's drawing tools, brushes, or filters. Use your Background layer to change the background color.

At this point, it's a good idea to save a copy of your layered repeat file in case you want to make color or design changes later on.

7 To define your pattern and create a pattern swatch, flatten all your layers in the layers palette and choose Select, All from the top menu. With your entire canvas selected, choose Edit, Define Pattern, name your pattern swatch, and select OK.

8 To test out your new pattern swatch, create a new document that's at least twice the size of your repeat tile, making sure the color mode and resolution are the same. Choose Select, All, then Edit, Fill. In the Fill option box, choose Pattern from the drop-down menu and select the Custom Pattern to reveal your swatch options. Choose your pattern and select OK.

9 Your canvas should now be filled with your new repeating tile design. If you need to make any adjustments, open your layered file and return to Step 7 to define your pattern and create a new pattern swatch.

5

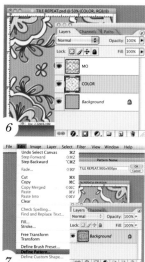

6

8

7

9

Half-drop repeat

1 Using the same motif, follow Steps 1 and 2 from the tile repeat tutorial to prepare your design file.

2 Create a new layer underneath your Motif layer and fill it with the background color of your design. Select both layers, choose Merge Layers from the layers palette, and duplicate your newly merged Motif layer. The duplicate layer will automatically be named Motif Copy.

3 Select Image, Canvas Size and double your original canvas width, keeping your height unchanged. For example, if your original canvas was 900 pixels wide by 900 pixels high, input 1,800 pixels wide x 900 pixels high. Choose the left-facing horizontal arrow in the Anchor orientation and select OK.

4 Select your Motif Copy layer and choose Filter, Other, Offset from the top menu. To create a half-drop repeat, your horizontal dimensions remain the same and your vertical dimensions are divided in half. For example, if your original canvas is 900 pixels wide x 900 pixels high, input Horizontal 900 pixels x Vertical 450 pixels. Choose Wrap Around in the Undefined Areas and select OK.

5 Follow Steps 5 through 9 from the tile-repeat tutorial (see page 29) to complete your design. Then create a new pattern swatch and test out your half-drop repeat.

1

3

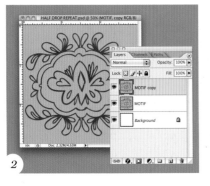

2

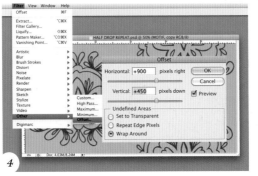

4

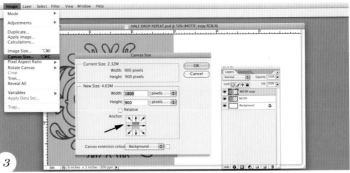

5

Brick repeat

1 Using the same motif, follow Steps 1 and 2 from the half-drop repeat tutorial (see page 30) to prepare your design file. Increase your canvas size by doubling your height and keeping your width unchanged. For example, if your original canvas was 900 pixels wide x 900 pixels high, input 900 pixels wide x 1,800 pixels high. Choose the vertical arrow in the Anchor orientation and select OK.

2 Select your Motif Copy layer and choose Filter, Other, Offset from the top menu. To create a brick repeat, your horizontal dimensions are divided in half and your vertical dimensions remain the same. For example, if your original canvas is 900 pixels wide x 900 pixels high, input Horizontal 450 pixels x Vertical 900 pixels. Select Wrap Around in the Undefined Areas and select OK.

3 Follow Steps 5 through 9 from the tile-repeat tutorial (see page 29) to complete your design. Then create a new pattern swatch and test out your new brick repeat.

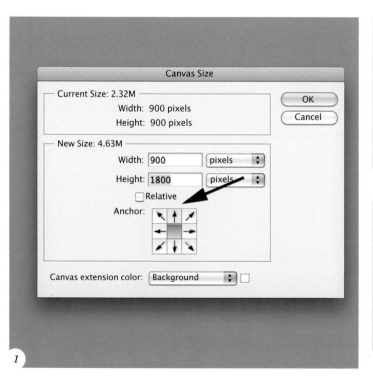

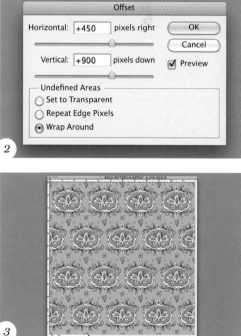

HEATHER DUTTON
Interview

Heather Dutton is a freelance surface and textile designer based in Maine. She studied fashion design at SCAD (The Savannah College of Art and Design) and after years of working in fashion in San Francisco, Heather went out on her own and launched Hang Tight Studios. She has worked with a broad range of clients, including Pottery Barn, Red Envelope, World Market, and JCPenney.

hangtightstudio.com

Describe your studio/work space.

After years of living and working in San Francisco, I relocated to the beautiful coastal town of Kennebunk, Maine, where I bought a great old house and quickly claimed the sunniest room for my studio space. Surrounded by windows with brightly painted lime-green walls, my studio feels light and happy even on the gloomiest winter days. My workspace is filled with all sorts of treasures that make me smile, including two kitties and my Sussex spaniel Emma Jean.

Are you formally trained as a designer?

I began my career as a fashion designer and the years that I spent working in the fashion industry were invaluable. I was fortunate enough to travel the world, work with a group of talented artists, and get an in-depth look at the creative processes of designing and manufacturing. Those experiences not only helped shape me as a designer, they also helped me realize my true passion for surface design.

"My studio feels light and happy even on the gloomiest winter days."

Summer Sweets oven mitt.

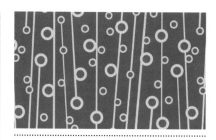

Berry Branch design.

> *"I love creating all types of designs, whether it's a regimented geometric, a silly whimsical creation, or a fancy floral design."*

Fabrics from Heather's Bloem Collection.

Do you consider yourself a generalist or a specialist?

I'd consider myself to be a generalist. I love creating all types of designs, whether it's a regimented geometric, a silly whimsical creation, or a fancy floral design. Working on a wide variety of designs helps feed the different facets of my personality and keeps me constantly inspired.

Do you generally work digitally or do you hand-draw your art? Or do you combine techniques?

All of my designs are created digitally but the initial ideas always start out in my sketchbook. Sometimes the sketches are just a loose idea for a pattern or collection and other times I end up using my original sketch in the finished design (thanks to Adobe Illustrator's Live Trace tool). I love the flexibility you get when you're creating a design digitally. I can easily play around with the layout, scale, or color, and sometimes I discover an unexpected direction for the design along the way.

Designs from Heather's Bonjour Lapin Collection.

What other creative pursuits do you practice?

When I'm not designing patterns, you're bound to find me behind my sewing machine whipping up all sorts of creations. I recently started sewing an assortment of free-form appliqué tea towels for my Etsy shop and retail stores (including shopSCAD). I also love to knit and I dabble with photography, even though I'm definitely a novice at both.

A transformed thrift-store chair with plump cushion made from Heather's Paisley fabric.

iPad case using Heather's Numero Uno fabric.

"When I'm feeling uninspired I know that it's time to get out of my studio and change my scenery. It could be something as simple as a walk on the beach, a quick trip down to Boston or New York, or a full-on trip to a far-off destination."

What do you do if you're feeling uninspired or stuck?

When I'm feeling uninspired I know that it's time to get out of my studio and change my scenery. It could be something as simple as a walk on the beach, a quick trip down to Boston or New York, or a full-on trip to a far-off destination. Traveling always wakes up my creative juices and makes me see things from a different perspective.

Are there any new techniques (not necessarily related to pattern design) you'd like to try?

If I had to pick one new technique that I wanted to learn, it would definitely be embroidery. I've always loved the way it looks. All those colorful threads and different textures make me giddy. I've purchased a few books and collected some supplies over the years, but I still haven't taken the plunge. I think it's about time!

A vintage-inspired apron created by Heather using her Fleur de Cuillère fabric.

How do you market your pattern design work?

Marketing your work is a vital part of being self-employed and there are so many resources out there to help you stay connected. One of the best resources I've found is Spoonflower.com. Not only has Spoonflower helped me connect with a large group of talented designers, it's also increased my visibility and brought about some really exciting design opportunities. I also use Facebook, Flickr, Etsy, and blog postings to help broaden my exposure. Without a doubt, all of these vehicles have dramatically impacted my business.

Do you have advice for someone who wants to try to design patterns professionally?

Having confidence in your work, marketing your designs, and creative networking (both professionally and personally) is key, especially if you plan on being self-employed. It's also important to keep up to date with trends and to stay connected to what's happening in the markets that you're designing for.

Fabrics from Heather's Dog-Gone It Collection.

Do you have advice for artists regarding how to market and sell their work?

Creating a website or blog to showcase your designs is paramount. You don't have to show all of your work, but it's important to at least give a taste of your design style and personality so potential clients can quickly get a feel for you and your work. Teaming up with a print studio or agency is also a great way to jump-start your design career and help you connect with your market early on.

What do you see next for you and your career?

I've been creating surface designs and illustrations for a variety of companies since I launched my freelance business, but you remain relatively anonymous with most contracted design work. I would love to expand the licensing end of my business, slowly step out from the shadows, and eventually develop name recognition within the industry.

Heather's Bursting Bloom design.

Throw pillow made from Heather's Chillout fabric.

3 PRINTING PATTERNS

by Amy Prior and Carly Schwerdt

Printing a pattern can be as simple as inking up a cut potato and printing it across fabric, or as challenging as printing an intricate allover pattern to create yardage. The nature of printing allows you to make multiples of your designs quickly, which is both satisfying and cost efficient.

Techniques such as screen printing, block printing, sun-dyeing, heat transfers, and drawing with pens and bleach are all simple yet very effective ways to create stunning patterns on fabric.

These processes can also be combined and layered with endless possibilities for creative and inspiring results. In a professional context, unique fabric designs can give you that designer edge.

Working with natural fabrics is a pleasure aesthetically, but is also a necessity with some printing techniques. Most inks, dyes, and transfer media require a natural fabric such as cotton, linen, silk, or hemp to give the best results. Where possible choose a natural fabric with a tight weave—if the weave is too open your inks may bleed, especially with screen printing. Most of the techniques in this chapter require heat setting and ironing flat before printing. Natural fibers like cotton, linen, and hemp can be ironed at high temperatures necessary to ensure the prints are set.

PRINTING YARDAGE

1 Tape your stencil under the silkscreen, making sure it is parallel to the base of the screen. Measure the repeat width of your stencil pattern; this is the distance between the first and second repeats. Note: this is not the width of your design, but the design plus the space where the next repeat starts. Write down this measurement.

2 Iron and pin the fabric to the felt underlay, check that both the underlay and fabric are parallel to the table edge. Apply a strip of masking tape parallel to the edge of your fabric and mark the noted repeat width measurement along the tape's length in pencil, beginning with R1 (Repeat 1), R2, R3, and so on for reference until you reach the end of your fabric piece. Place the edge of your silkscreen along the masking tape to the right of your first pencil mark.

TOOLS AND MATERIALS

- Masking tape
- Paper or craft knife
- Cut water-resistant paper stencil (in repeat)
- Silkscreen
- Ruler
- Pencil and paper
- Iron
- Pins
- Fabric
- Felt underlay
- Ink knife or spatula
- Squeegee
- Water-soluble fabric ink

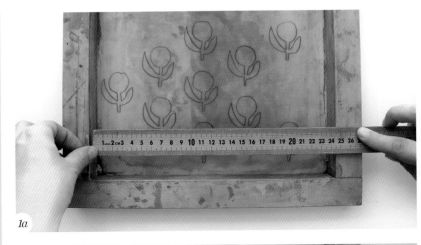

1a

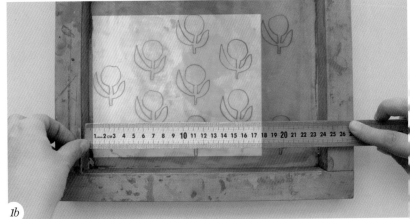

1b

Hints and tips

To print full width yardage with this method, it is easiest to use a large screen and stencil. Otherwise, with a small screen you will need to make your stencil pattern repeat both side to side and top and bottom and print two or more rows of pattern, which will interconnect to achieve full widths of printed pattern.

3 Print each alternate repeat beginning with odd numbers: 1, 3, 5, etc. Wash and dry your screen.

4 Let the fabric air dry, then go back to fill the even intervals: 2, 4, 6, etc. This ensures that no ink is transferred by the edges of your silkscreen while printing. Your print will now appear as a complete pattern length. Wash and dry the screen. Let your fabric dry for twenty-four hours and then iron hot to fix.

3

4

SCREEN-PRINTING OVERVIEW

Reusable Stencil

1 Draw your design or pattern onto the acetate film. For accuracy, you may wish to pre-draw your design, then trace it onto the acetate. Use a sharp craft knife to cut your shapes out on a cutting mat. The parts you cut out will be the shapes where the ink will print.

2 Mask the edges of your silkscreen with tape. The ink will not pass through the tape. Make sure the acetate is bigger than the masked area so that no ink will bleed through.

3 Use paper to protect the underside of the printed surface if you are using a product with layers such as a cushion, bag, or skirt. Place your stencil onto the printing surface, i.e. bag, fabric, or cushion, and place the screen over the top. Make sure no part of the cut pattern is under the tape.

4 With a butter knife, spread a generous amount of ink in a line across the masked area of your screen.

TOOLS AND MATERIALS
- Pencil
- Acetate film
- Natural fabric
- Craft knife
- Cutting mat
- Masking tape/sticky tape
- Paper
- Silkscreen
- Black marker
- Butter knife or spatula
- Fabric screen-printing ink
- Squeegee

Hints and tips

Remember to keep the pieces you cut out of your acetate; you can use them to print your pattern in reverse.

Adding registration marks in black marker will help you to line everything up.

5 Now place the squeegee edge onto the screen above the ink. Glide the squeegee firmly down the screen toward you, holding the squeegee at a 45-degree angle. Make sure that all of your pattern is covered in ink. Pull your squeegee three times to get good coverage. The final pull should be firm enough to collect all the extra ink from the screen.

6 Holding the printed surface down, carefully lift the screen from one side. The ink should make the stencil stick to the screen, enabling you to print again if you want to.

7 Wash your screen immediately with cold running water to remove all ink from the screen surface, the frame, and the stencil surface. Dried ink can clog the screen permanently. Wooden-handled squeegees need to be wiped with a soft cloth; do not leave them in water.

8 Leave your printed item to air dry for twelve hours and then heat set with a hot iron for three minutes or as per the instructions on the ink.

5

6

7

SCREEN-PRINTING TEXTURES

Hints and tips

You can choose many other items to create beautiful textures through a screen, such as string, rubber bands, cut paper shapes, leaves, wire mesh, and ripped paper.

Even an old, damaged silkscreen with residual ink and leftover areas of emulsion can be printed through for a wonderfully rustic texture.

TOOLS AND MATERIALS

- Tissue paper confetti
- Natural base cloth
- Felt underlay
- Silkscreen
- Water-based fabric ink
- Ink knife or spatula
- Knife
- Squeegee

1 Randomly sprinkle the tissue paper confetti over your ironed base cloth, which has been laid onto your felt underlay printing surface. Separate some of the larger clumps of confetti and move pieces around to achieve your desired density and arrangement.

2 Slowly place silkscreen over the confetti. Place ink along the top of your screen with a knife or spatula.

3 Firmly pull ink over the screen at least four times with a very firm last pull to remove any excess ink from the screen and the fabric print below it.

4 Gently lift the screen from one end to reveal a solid background with circles. Sometimes the confetti inks bleed to the edges of each circle, creating a beautiful effect. Use the squeegee to wash the ink and confetti from your screen. Carefully pull off any confetti left behind on your printed fabric. Let the fabric dry for twenty-four hours and iron hot to fix.

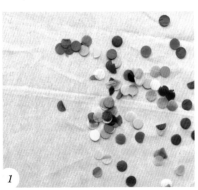

BLOCK PRINTING

Hints and tips

Varying the pressure when printing enables you to create lighter and darker areas from one block.

TOOLS AND MATERIALS

- Easy Carve print block (or a wood or linoleum block)
- Pencil
- Lino carving tools
- Fabric printing ink
- Ink roller
- Inking knife or spatula
- Glass or plastic mat
- Felt underlay
- Ironed natural base cloth

1   Draw or trace your design onto the Easy Carve print block with pencil. Carve around or into your design; remember that the surfaces you want to print are the parts that are left uncut.

2   Roll a small amount of ink onto the glass or plastic mat until it is evenly distributed. Stamp the carved surface firmly onto the inky surface to collect ink.

3   Place the felt underlay onto the table surface and position the ironed base cloth on top. Firmly press the inked block face down onto the cloth. Re-ink the block and repeat to create an overall pattern.

4   Wash and dry your block between color changes. Let the fabric dry for twenty-four hours and iron hot to fix.

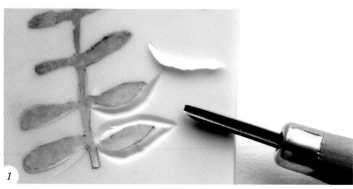

2

1

3

HEAT-TRANSFER PRINTING

Hints and tips

Use lots of crayon for brighter, more intense colors

TOOLS AND MATERIALS

- White office paper
- Fabric wax crayons
- Iron
- Natural base cloth

1 Draw, shade, or rub your design onto paper with fabric wax crayons.

2 Turn the paper face down onto the natural base cloth where you would like your print to go. Hot iron the back of the paper. Keep your iron moving so as not to burn the paper.

3 Lift up the paper from one corner to reveal your design, now transferred onto your fabric. Launder the fabric according to crayon manufacturer directions.

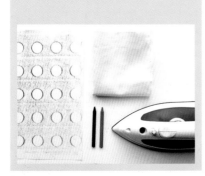

2

1

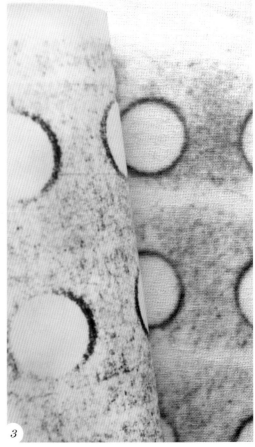
3

IRON-ON TRANSFER PRINTING

Hints and tips

Any text-based imagery will need to be printed in reverse so that it will be the right way round when it is transferred onto fabric.

TOOLS AND MATERIALS

- Paper scissors
- Iron-on transfer paper printed with an image or design from an ink-jet printer (see manufacturer's instructions)
- Lightly printed fabric or plain fabric
- Iron
- Natural base cloth

1   Cut right up to and around the edge of your ink-jet printed image.

2   Position your cut image onto the desired area of your fabric, with the picture facing down. Hot iron according to the manufacturer's instructions.

3   Gently peel back the iron-on paper to reveal your image now transferred onto your fabric. Launder the fabric according to transfer paper manufacturer directions.

2

1

3

FABRIC/ BLEACH PEN

Hints and tips

The bleach can bleed, so keep your design simple, and draw with lines and dots rather than filling in large areas.

Using fabric markers and bleach pens, you can add and take away color to create new looks.

TOOLS AND MATERIALS

- Patterned or plain fabric
- Colored fabric
- Fabric markers
- Iron
- Bleach pen

1   Add color to your chosen fabric by drawing on it with fabric markers. Hot iron to set.

2   Bleach pens need to be used with care; children should be supervised and you should only work in a well-ventilated area.

3   Shake the bleach pen and do a test on a piece of sample fabric before starting to draw—the pen will take away color from colored or printed fabrics. Machine or hand wash.

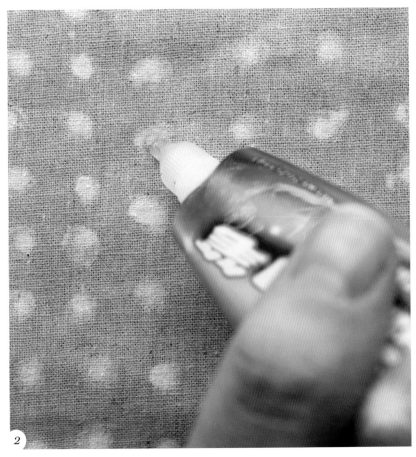

1

2

SUN DYEING

Hints and tips

Sun dyes are available in primary colors that can be mixed to create a full spectrum to enjoy.

Lay the fabric onto a piece of cardboard to keep it sturdy while it's outside.

TOOLS AND MATERIALS

- Paintbrush
- Light-sensitive dyes (Inkodye by Lumi was used here)
- Fabric
- Paper
- Scissors
- Cardboard (optional)
- Hot, soapy water

1 Dip your brush into the dye and paint directly onto your fabric.

2 Place objects or cut paper shapes on top of your painted imagery if white areas are desired.

3 Take the fabric into sunlight for ten minutes to expose the ink until it darkens or has reached the desired intensity of color.

4 Remove the paper shapes (or objects) right before washing the fabric vigorously in hot soapy water to "fix" the image.

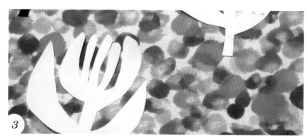

PRINTING
PATTERNS

Gallery

Fox pillow. Organic cotton screen-printed with water-based inks, hand-stuffed and sewn. By Shannon Kennedy of Sass & Peril

Original painting of wheat design digitally printed on a silk collar. Collaboration by Angie Johnson and Jen Storey

Lion pillow. Organic cotton screen-printed with water-based inks, hand-stuffed and sewn. By Shannon Kennedy of Sass & Peril

Novel Idea. Pair of handstamped fabric bookends made from natural bull denim and water-based printers ink. Original design by Joshua By Oak by Debra Williamson

Handbag made with hand screen-printed fabric. Birdcage fabric by Sarah Waterhouse. By Jennifer Ladd

Bike fabric by Hollabee. By Jennifer Ladd

Handbag made with hand screen-printed fabric. Tulip fabric by Chomp. By Jennifer Ladd

Screen-printed fabric yardage in Akzidenz design. By Susan Fitzgerald

Hand screen-printed pillow cover on reproduction bark cloth. By Erin Flett

Contemporary folk-art owl doll hand painted on quilter's muslin. By Jo James and Dylan Curry

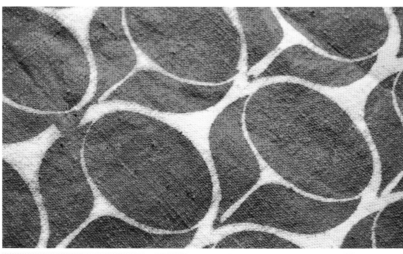

Canvas fabric printed with hand-cut freezer paper stencil. By Emily LeBaron

Pink Cassette Tape. Screen printed and handmade cotton pillow. By Mimi Oeberg

Hand screen-printed pillow cover on reproduction bark cloth. By Erin Flett

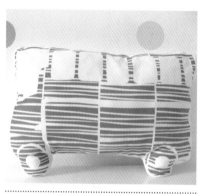

Autobus pillow in Tebraria design. Hand screen-printed using freezer paper. By Eva Reisinger

Everywhere Silverware. Original drawing hand-drawn with wax crayons. Scanned and digitally printed on linen cotton canvas using Spoonflower.com. By Anja Hanschmann

Soft toy made from screen-printed fabric. By Susan Fitzgerald

UMBRELLA PRINTS

Interview

Umbrella Prints is an Australian textile house run by Amy Prior and Carly Schwerdt. They produce two lines of fabric: hand screen-printed on organic base cloth and a printed quilter's weight cotton. Known for their lovely patterns, Umbrella Prints has been producing fabric since 2006.

umbrellaprints.com.au

"Our patterns are a unique mix of super graphic shape and illustrative lines and textures "

Carly Schwerdt.

Amy Prior.

Where are you located?
We work from Nest Studio
in Stepney, South Australia.

**Can you describe
your studio work space?**
Lots of light, children, color,
and music. It is a happy and busy space.

Are you formally trained as artists?

We both have honors degrees in our fields; Carly as a graphic designer and Amy as an artist/printmaker.

Do you consider yourselves generalists or specialists?

Both; we specialize in fabric design but we're generally interested and capable in other creative areas such as product design, painting, styling, photography, and drawing.

What techniques and materials do you generally use?

We are open to all techniques and materials. For example we might create a block and print by hand onto paper and then create a repeat on the computer. A computer, a large table, and a wide range of mark-making tools are indispensable. Usually our art becomes the basis of a textile design rather than "right, let's design a pattern on the computer." Our patterns are a unique mix of super graphic shape, and illustrative lines and textures; we often play with our favorite designs in terms of scale and repeat. Color is a passion. We want every inch of the fabric to be beautiful, which is why people keep coming back to buy our trimmings and remnants packs.

How did you start your business and how has it grown?

We met seven years ago in the doorway of two neighboring shops we were working from. We just really clicked creatively and have a similar sense of taste and humor. Initially we decided to be quite fluid with our approach, to see where the business naturally took us, but now we like to focus more on fabric design rather than design products with fabrics. Pattern has always been the heart of what we do.

Patchwork pieces by Umbrella Prints.

Grand Hearts fabric in Bosc Pear; reupholstered mid-century Danish chair.

How do you market and sell your products?

We have a website and an online shop, as well as an outlet on Etsy. We also have a select group of retailers who support us and sell our fabrics. We have been very fortunate through word of mouth. The Umbrella Prints Trimmings competition has been a huge success every year and is fun for our customers.

How often do you release a new collection?

We release our screen-printed fabrics one by one and reprint when necessary and in different colors as we fancy; the focus here is not on the new but on the classic. Our quilters cotton ranges come out twice a year. We don't pre-set a specific number of designs or colorways. We don't print it if we're not feeling it.

What do you do if you're feeling uninspired or stuck?

We relish any moment to design and never feel uninspired. The reality of running a business though is that administration takes up a lot of our time and can be boring. We rely on coffee, breaks, and just sheer persistence to get it done.

Umbrella Prints at Nest Studio

"We release our screen-printed fabrics one by one and reprint when necessary and in different colors as we fancy; the focus here is not on the new but on the classic."

How do you collaborate on your design work?

We chat back and forth about color choices, repeat styles, and size; so although a design might originate from the lines or shapes of one of us, it generally morphs into a collaboration by the time it is resolved for print.

What advice would you offer someone who wants to try screen printing?

Just try it! All you need is a table, a screen, a squeegee, paper, tape, a knife, and ink. You don't need to train or study or buy elaborate equipment (though you might like to later). Don't get hung up on perfect repeats and ruling lines to begin with. Have fun, make a mess, and trust your eyes.

Are there any new techniques you'd like to try?

Amy: I love drawing, so I'm keen to experiment more with fabric pens and markers to create one-off artworks. Carly: The Inkodyes are so much fun, I'd like to see how far I can take their application onto different surfaces.

Umbrella Prints' quilters cotton range.

"Don't get hung up on perfect repeats and ruling lines. Have fun, make a mess, and trust your eyes."

Umbrella Prints' Trimmings: a unique mix of beautiful color and pattern.

CYANOTYPE

by Christina McFall

Cyanotype is a photographic process that uses sunlight to print an image. The distinctive blue of a cyanotype print is dyed into the fabric, leaving the hand and texture unchanged. And since it's photographic, you can print with a full tonal range—anything from graphic art to photographs.

To make a cyanotype print, simply coat your chosen fabric with the cyanotype sensitizer, let it dry, and then expose it to sunlight with your artwork negative placed on top. Where the negative is clear, the fabric will turn blue, where the negative blocks the sunlight it will remain the background color, and translucent areas will produce corresponding shades of blue.

Cyanotype is a versatile technique and is particularly well suited for printing on heavily textured fabrics, such as corduroy, felt, or even hand-knits. To print, the fabric must have some absorbent fiber content to hold the dye, and cyanotype works best with cotton, linen, rayon, bamboo, and silk.

Cyanotype fabric, watercolor paper, thread, and running stitch. By Suzanne Harlow

The Organic Garden quilt. Cyanotypes on cotton, artist-painted and commercial cotton and silk fabric, and machine stitching. Original art and photography by Sue Reno

While the classic cyanotype is blue, it's easy to incorporate color by printing on colored or pre-printed fabric. You can also convert the blue to a few different colors through a process called toning.

The basic cyanotype kit is inexpensive and can be ordered through photo supply shops; pre-treated fabric for printing is also available. As with all printing methods, always wear gloves and take care when handling and disposing of the chemicals.

Poke Salad quilt. Cyanotype on cotton, Indian silk fabrics, hand embroidery, machine stitching, and hand bead work. By Sue Reno

Big Root Geranium quilt. Cyanotypes on silk, artist-painted and commercial silk and cotton fabric, couched threads, machine stitching, and hand bead work. Art and photography by Sue Reno

CYANOTYPE PRINTING

1   Before you begin cyanotype printing, you need to create a digital negative of your artwork. To do this, open your digital artwork file and do the following: convert to grayscale, invert the colors, and flip the image from left-to-right. Your file is now ready to print onto the ink-jet transparency film to create your digital negative. Alternatively, you can prepare artwork by drawing directly on a sheet of acetate with an opaque black marker. Or, you can use objects like leaves and lace to create shadowgrams.

2   Next, gather your supplies and find a workspace that has no sunlight (ordinary indoor lights are fine). Wear gloves and protect yourself and your workspace from the cyanotype solution, which can leave dark blue stains. Following the instructions in the cyanotype kit, mix the two stock solutions in the provided bottles. Then, using the measuring cup, mix equal parts of stock solution A and solution B together to create the active cyanotype sensitizer. Mix only as much as needed to coat fabric for this session, as the active sensitizer will only last about thirty minutes. A good starting estimate is to mix a total of 2 tbsp (30ml) of sensitizer per square foot/meter of fabric.

TOOLS AND MATERIALS

- Ink-jet transparency film
- Cyanotype kit (with bottles)
- Gloves
- Measuring cup
- Pre-washed fabric
- Foam brush
- Muslin cloth, scrap piece (optional)
- Plastic clips
- Black bag, lightproof (optional)
- Picture frame (glass and backing)
- Tape or binder clips (optional)
- UV lamp (optional)
- Washtub
- Hydrogen peroxide

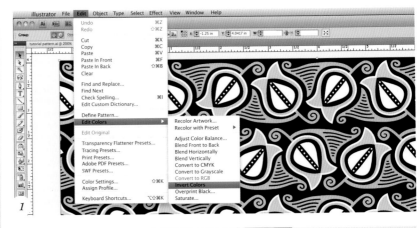

1

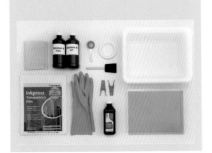

2

Hints and tips

For best results, use natural fiber fabrics such as cotton, linen, rayon, and silk.

Pre-wash your fabric to remove any sizing or dirt.

Experiment with different colors and unusual textures of fabric. Use thicker lines in your artwork for heavily textured fabrics.

3 Using a clean foam brush, carefully coat your dry pre-washed fabric with the cyanotype sensitizer. You only need to coat the area where you want to print. Alternatively, you can immerse the piece of fabric in a tray of sensitizer to completely saturate it, but this can be difficult for larger pieces. If you have over-saturated the fabric, use a scrap piece of muslin cloth to blot away the excess. Avoid wringing it as this can warp the fabric. Ideally you want the fabric to be evenly coated, but not so saturated that it will drip.

4 Hang the sensitized fabric to dry in a completely dark area, such as a closet. Use plastic clips and protect the floor from any drips, which could stain. When the fabric is completely dry, place it in a lightproof black bag for storage until you are ready to print. For best results, use the fabric within two weeks.

3

4

CYANOTYPE
PRINTING

5   When you have a clear, sunny day and are ready to print, assemble the contact printing frame as follows: place the coated fabric flat on top of the backing board, arrange the digital negative on top with the ink side down, and place the sheet of glass on top. You can use tape or binder clips to keep the negative and fabric from shifting out of alignment. Assemble the printing frame indoors and away from strong sunlight.

6   Carry the assembled printing frame outside and place in full sunlight, with the surface tilted toward the sun. Exposure times vary depending on the intensity of the sunlight and will range from five to twenty minutes. You will know the print is fully exposed when the fabric under the clear areas of the negative has turned dark blue and then progressed to a silvery-gray color. Practice with a test piece of fabric to determine the exact time needed.

5

6

Hints and tips

If it's the wrong time of year for sunny days, you can also expose cyanotype prints with a UV lamp.

Add a small amount of white vinegar to your first rinse water to increase the depth of the blue tones.

7 After exposing, bring the printing frame back indoors before disassembling. Fill the washtub with cold tap water and submerge the exposed fabric in the water. Agitate gently and watch as the dark blue tones develop and the yellow sensitizer washes away. Keep rinsing until most of the yellow has rinsed out.

8 With the fabric still in the tub of water, add a splash of ordinary hydrogen peroxide to instantly darken the blues and bring out the contrast. This optional step speeds up the oxidation process that would happen naturally as the print aged. Change the water and continue rinsing in running water for ten minutes. Proper rinsing is critical to ensure a long-lasting print. Dry and iron according to the fabric instructions.

7

8

ADVANCED CYANOTYPE TONING

1 Make the two toning gels and put each in a squeeze bottle. To make the Yellow Gel: wearing gloves, measure ½ tsp (2 ml) soda ash into the measuring cup, add 2 fl oz (60 ml) hot water and stir with the stick until dissolved. Add ½ tsp (2 ml) sodium alginate thickener, let it stand for five to ten minutes to thicken, and transfer to a squeeze bottle. Add more or less thickener, as needed. Label this bottle Yellow Gel. To make the Brown Gel: repeat the same process using ½ tsp (2 ml) tannic acid powder, 2 fl oz (60 ml) hot water, and ½ tsp (2 ml) sodium alginate thickener. Take care with the tannic acid powder, as it can stain. Label this bottle Brown Gel.

2 Plan which areas of the print to tone yellow or brown. Yellow toning is created by applying the Yellow Gel, while brown toning is a two-step process that requires applying the Yellow Gel and then the Brown Gel. Apply the Yellow Gel to all the areas you want to tone yellow or brown. The coated areas will turn completely yellow within two minutes. Use the store-bought dye-resist paste to outline and protect areas you do not want to tone.

TOOLS AND MATERIALS

- Gloves
- Measuring spoons
- Soda ash (sodium carbonate)
- Measuring cup
- Stir stick
- Tannic acid powder
- Sodium alginate thickener
- Two plastic squeeze bottles
- Cyanotype print, washed and dry
- Dye-resist paste
- Cardstock or paper towel

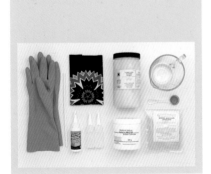

1

2

Hints and tips

The darkest blues will create the richest yellows and browns when toning.

Try using shibori or stenciling to apply the toning gels.

Yellow toning is best on white fabric, but brown works on many colors.

Apply tannic acid directly to blue areas to create a blue-black tone.

3 Remove the excess Yellow Gel by gently wiping it away with small pieces of cardstock or paper towel. Be very careful to avoid smearing the gel into other areas or they will also turn yellow.

4 Apply dye-resist paste to areas that you want to remain yellow in order to protect them from the Brown Gel applied in the next step. You do not need to let the resist dry, since this is only temporary coverage.

5 Next, apply the Brown Gel to the yellow areas that you want to tone brown. When the brown has darkened enough (one to two minutes), wipe off the excess Brown Gel, being careful not to contaminate other areas. To rinse, hold the fabric under running water and quickly wash off any remaining Yellow or Brown Gel to minimize secondary staining. Then proceed to rinse away the remaining resist paste. Wash the fabric very thoroughly in plain water and dry.

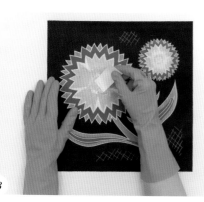

3

4

5

CHRISTINA MCFALL

Interview

Christina McFall is obsessed with color, texture, form, and chemical reactions. She approaches her art with the mind of a scientist, carefully recording tests and cataloging results. Using cyanotype printing, she harnesses UV light to create Prussian Blue prints on fabric. Originally from California, she is now based in Berlin, Germany.

christinamcfall.com

What techniques and materials do you generally use?

Cyanotype printing is an old photographic technique that uses sunlight to print your artwork onto sensitized fabric in a blue dye. I typically use digital negatives of my artwork and like to experiment with different colors and textures by printing on fabrics such as linen, hand knits, corduroy, and cotton.

Are you formally trained as an artist?

I studied art in college and earned my BFA in photography and film, back in the days before digital took over. This is where I was first introduced to cyanotype printing on paper. I was quickly enchanted by it, mainly because I loved the hands-on nature of this method. For the past few years I've been specializing in cyanotypes on fabric, experimenting with techniques and a variety of different textiles.

> *"After working in the corporate world for several years, I found myself longing to do something more creative and in 2010 I finally took the leap."*

Pillow with toned cyanotype design on pink corduroy.

Pillow with cyanotype-printed squirrel design on preprinted cotton.

Hotpad with cyanotype-printed bunny design on white linen.

"At heart I am a generalist, because I could never dedicate myself to only one discipline."

Do you consider yourself a generalist or a specialist?

At heart I am a generalist, because I could never dedicate myself to only one discipline. I enjoy trying my hand at lots of different crafts and techniques, exploring the different capabilities, and reaching a certain level of mastery with each.

Can you describe your studio/work space?

Since cyanotype printing can be messy, I have separate dry and wet work areas. I do all my designing and sewing in the comfort of my home studio. Then I do the cyanotype printing and processing in my darkroom where I have a big sink and don't have to worry about making a mess. I also expose my prints in my darkroom with a custom-built UV lightbox, since I can't rely on the sun year-round.

How do you market and sell your products?

I currently market my handprinted items online through Etsy and my website. Etsy is a great place to get started, to test market products, and watch for trends. I've also found that teaching classes and attending craft fairs is wonderful for networking and generating awareness. I also teach hands-on cyanotype printing courses at local art studios.

Can you briefly describe how you started your business and how it's grown since its inception?

After working in the corporate world for several years, I found myself longing to do something more creative and in 2010 I finally took the leap and started my own craft business. In the beginning, I focused only on selling my handprinted goods, but now I'm expanding more and more into writing tutorials and teaching workshops.

Horse ornament with cyanotype-printed design on blue felt.

Book cover with cyanotype-printed design on red linen.

Where do you find inspiration?

My creativity is often sparked by traditional folk and decorative arts from various cultures and eras. I'm particularly drawn to motifs that echo the natural world, and these themes influence my own original designs. For inspiration I like to visit museums and libraries, read vintage magazines, and browse sites like archive.org and the Victoria and Albert Museum online.

What advice would you offer someone who wants to try cyanotype?

Buy a kit, choose a sunny day and start printing—it's as easy as that! Digital negatives can be tricky, so for your first prints I recommend using whatever you have on hand: leaves and flowers from the garden, paper cutouts, glassware, old film negatives, lace, etc. You will be amazed how quickly you pick up the process and start to make beautiful prints.

"Buy a kit, choose a sunny day and start printing— it's as easy as that!"

Pre-printed cotton fabric overprinted with cyanotype design.

Dress with cyanotype-printed whale design on green striped seersucker.

Pencil pouches with cyanotype-printed floral design on blue and pink corduroy.

"For your first prints I recommend using whatever you have on hand: leaves and flowers from the garden, paper cutouts, glassware, old film negatives, lace, etc."

Are there any new techniques you'd like to try?

I've always wanted to try traditional indigo dyeing with shibori techniques. I'm fascinated by all the clever shibori methods for making different patterns, and it would be fun to learn a few while also learning how to use indigo dye.

What do you see next f or your design/art career?

I'm excited that I have recently relocated from California to Berlin. This is a great opportunity and I'm looking forward to becoming active in the local arts community. I pleasantly anticipate that my designs will reflect new influences as I explore European sights and cultures, and I intend to blog all about it.

Woven cotton scarf with cyanotype-printed design.

E-reader sleeve with toned cyanotype photograph on khaki linen.

Pre-printed cotton fabric overprinted with cyanotype design.

Crocheted potholder in orange cotton yarn with cyanotype-printed design.

4 DYEING AND BLEACHING

by Sara Hopp

Creating your own fabric is extremely rewarding, and often addictive. Although they can be messy, the techniques in this chapter aren't hard to master. You can create a rich and interesting surface with any single dyeing or bleaching method, or by mixing and layering different techniques. An open mind and willingness to experiment are key, since there is always an element of unpredictability when working with dye and bleach; that is what makes these processes so exciting!

Dyeing is the process of chemically bonding dye molecules to the fibers of your fabric. Using dye is akin to using transparent watercolors, so it's helpful to keep color mixing in mind as you're layering dyes and techniques. Pattern can be created by using resists, which block dye from contact with certain areas of fabric, or by removing color in selected areas using discharge paste or bleach.

This chapter focuses on adding and removing color to plant-based cellulose fibers. Wool and silk can also be used, but may require extra steps. Working with synthetic fabrics is not recommended since they often give unpredictable or unsatisfactory results. For more information on dyeing, see the Dyeing Charts on pages 164–165.

SAFETY AND WORKING WITH DYES AND BLEACH

Creating a dye box

Although generally safe, dyes and auxiliaries are somewhat toxic in powdered form so it is a good precaution to work with a dye box when you are measuring. A dye box can help to reduce the spread of powered dye into the area you are working in. To make a dye box, cut one side off a cardboard box so you have a three-sided box. Line the bottom and sides with newspaper. Before measuring any dye, lightly mist the paper so that it is damp. The damp paper will catch any spilled particles so they don't become airborne.

You can safely dispose of dyebaths in a household drain, making sure that you do not contaminate pets, children, or plants. Let the faucet run for five minutes to dilute any chemicals.

Treating fabric before and after dyeing

Before dyeing or discharging, wash fabric in hot water and textile detergent to remove dirt or debris. Skipping this step can result in a blotchy finished product. If you dry fabric in a dryer, do not use fabric softener as it can interfere with dye or bleach solutions.

Depending on the technique you've used, you may need to batch your fabric. Batching is a process whereby you let the fabric sit in a warm and humid environment for two to twenty-four hours to allow the chemical reaction to fully exhaust itself. Place the dyed fabric in a clean container. Cover the container with an inverted container of a larger size or with plastic wrap. Place the container in a warm area until batching is completed.

Once your fabric has been dyed and batching is finished (if applicable), you need to remove excess dye and chemicals. Wash using textile detergent, dry, and press as desired.

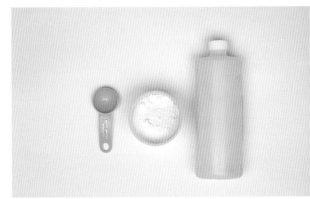

Safety

- Dyeing can be messy so dress appropriately.
- Cover your workspace with a plastic cloth or kraft paper to avoid stains and make clean-up easier.
- Wear gloves because dyes, auxiliary chemicals, and bleach can irritate your skin.
- Work in a well-ventilated area.

- Wear a respirator with cartridges for particles and eye protection.
- Do not use tools (measuring spoons, containers, etc.) that are also used for food preparation.
- Store dyes and chemicals where pets or children will not have access to them.

Chemical solutions

Depending on the technique you are using, you may need to mix urea water and dye activator solutions.

Urea water—used to make the dye solution in techniques such as tie-dye and dip dyeing, where the dye is applied directly to specific areas of the fabric. Mix ½ cup (120 ml) of urea with 2 cups (480 ml) of water. Stir until thoroughly dissolved. You can keep urea water in a covered container for a couple of weeks for later use, but you should discard it if you notice an odor of ammonia.

Dye activator soak—fabric is soaked in this solution when the dye is applied directly to certain areas of the fabric. This helps to fix the dye just to that area. To prepare the solution, mix ½ cup (120 ml) soda ash or dye activator with 2 qt (2 l) water until dissolved. Soda ash soak can be re-used and will keep indefinitely in a covered container or bucket.

MAKING NATURAL DYES

1   Decide how much fabric you will be dyeing to determine how much mordant and dyestuff you will need. (See Natural Dyes chart on page 164.)

2   Before dyeing you'll need to add mordant to your fabric. Mordant creates the permanent bond between the dye molecules and the fiber. In a clean cup, dissolve the appropriate amount of alum and cream of tartar in warm water. Add this solution to your pot and add enough water to cover your fabric.

3   Add the fabric, place the pot over your heat source, bring to a simmer, and simmer for one hour. Allow the fabric to cool in the solution, then remove it, squeeze out the excess water, and discard the solution. You can allow the fabric to dry if you want to stockpile some pre-mordanted material, but it is best to use it within a month because alum can degrade the fabric over time.

TOOLS AND MATERIALS

- Pre-scoured cellulose fabric, preferably cotton
- Measuring spoons
- Mordant (alum and cream of tartar are the most versatile and least toxic)
- Clean cup and stainless steel or enamel dye pot (do not use a cup or pot that is also used for food or drink)
- Natural dyestuff
- Warm water
- Plastic containers
- Heat source (in order to simmer your fabric)
- Stirring tools

3

4

Hints and tips

Natural dyes generally give muted tones on plant-based (cellulose) fibers, such as cotton, and more brilliant colors on protein-based fibers, such as wool and silk.

Do not assume that because the dyes are derived from natural sources that natural dyeing is not toxic; mordants, in particular, can be dangerous both to you and the environment.

In this tutorial I focus on dyeing cotton (cellulose-based) fabric. Wool fabric or yarn can also be dyed with natural dyes, but avoid sudden temperature changes and agitation during the dyeing and rinsing steps, or the wool will felt. Synthetic fabrics don't produce good results.

Refer to the chart on page 164 for a list of some of the most frequently used natural dyestuffs and the colors that result when using alum and cream of tartar as mordants.

....

4 Next, make your dyebath. In many cases you can do this step while you mordant your fabric, although for the darkest shades, you may want to soak roots or large pieces overnight. Measure your dyestuff. You may need to chop up larger roots, such as madder. Add enough water to wet or dissolve the dyestuff as applicable, and add to a clean pot. Add water to cover your fabric and simmer for one hour, adding water as needed. Allow the solution to cool and strain out roots or shavings if necessary.

5 Now you're ready to dye the fabric. Add the wet, mordanted fabric to the dye solution, add water to cover if necessary, and bring to a simmer. Simmer for one hour. Do not allow the dyebath to boil.

6 Periodically stir or turn the fabric while it simmers to produce the most even color. Be sure not to splash yourself!

7 Turn off the heat and allow the solution to cool. The color will continue to penetrate the fibers during the cooling, so continue to stir or turn the fabric periodically. Remove the fabric and rinse. You can dispose of the dyebath, or save and re-use it to create lighter shades. Finish fabric according to the instructions on pages 70–71.

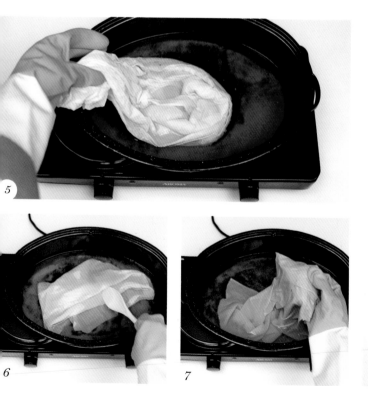

MIXING CHEMICAL DYEBATHS AND SOLUTIONS

1 Decide how much fabric you will be dyeing and determine how much salt, urea, dye, and start water you will need. Fill a plastic container or bucket with enough water to cover your fabric. Submerge the fabric and allow it to soak. (See Chemical Dyebaths chart on page 165.)

2 Using warm water, measure the start water into the container you will use for dyeing. Add the salt and urea and mix until dissolved.

3 Now mix the dye solution. Measure the dye powder into a plastic cup. Measure 2 cups (480 ml) of warm water into a separate cup. Add a very small amount of the water to the dye and stir to form a paste. Add more water little by little, if necessary. Some colors are more difficult to dissolve than others, so be patient. Once the powder is thoroughly dissolved, add the remaining water and mix thoroughly.

TOOLS AND MATERIALS

- Start water
- Dye activator
- Procion MX dyes
- Plastic measuring cups with pour spouts
- Plastic measuring spoons
- Plastic spoons
- Plastic cups for mixing
- Non-corrosive stirring tool
- Two medium plastic containers or buckets (12–27 qt/11.3–25.5 l)
- Dye box
- Salt
- Urea
- Water

1

2

3

Hints and tips

Around forty-five minutes in the dyebath consistently produces good results for most colors. The only exceptions are turquoise or blends containing turquoise, which benefit from remaining in the dyebath for up to twenty-four hours.

4   Add the dye solution to the container with the salt and urea solution.

5   Remove your fabric from the soaking water and squeeze to drain. Add the wet fabric to the dyebath and agitate gently. Carefully press out any air bubbles.

6   Measure the activator into a clean cup, add 1 cup (240 ml) of warm water and stir to dissolve. Carefully remove the fabric from the dyebath and place in a clean container. Pour the activator solution into the dyebath and stir. Put the fabric back into the bath and press out any air bubbles.

7   Let the fabric soak in the dyebath for forty-five minutes. Gently stirring, turning, and pressing the fabric will produce more even results. Leaving it alone will create a mottled effect.

8   Now you're ready to rinse. Fill a clean plastic container or bucket with clean, cool water. Pull your fabric from the dyebath, letting the excess dye solution drain. Transfer the fabric to the clean water bath and agitate gently with your gloved hand. Let it soak for a few minutes while you dispose of your dyebath (see page 70 for tips on proper disposal). Dump the rinse water, refill with clean water, and agitate again. Repeat as many times as necessary until the fabric feels clean, even though dye may still be running from it. Process according to the instructions on pages 70–71.

4

6

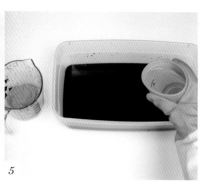

5

7

BLEACHING

Dip/vat

1 Prepare the bleach bath. In one container, start with a 50/50 ratio of bleach to water. For an allover effect, you'll need to have enough liquid in the bath so that your fabric can move freely. For a dip technique, use a shallow bath.

2 In a second container, mix neutralizer to manufacturer directions. Fill a third container with water for your rinse bath. Make sure to have enough neutralizer solution and rinse water so the fabric can move freely.

3 Now your baths are ready.

4 Test fabric scraps by dipping them into the bleach bath to gauge the bleach intensity and results. The color of the fabric should change within a minute or so. If the color changes too quickly, add more water. If the color changes very slowly, add bleach in ½–1 cup (120–240 ml) increments to preserve the integrity of the fibers as well as to give more control over the final result. You want to use the weakest solution that will produce satisfactory results because bleach can damage the fibers.

TOOLS AND MATERIALS

- Fabric: hand-dyed or commercial cotton, linen, or rayon. Note: this process will damage protein fibers (silk, wool). Synthetic fabrics do not yield consistent results.
- Non-corrosive measuring cup and spoons
- Three small (6–12 qt/5.5–11.3 l) plastic containers
- Household bleach
- Neutralizer (Anti-Chlor)
- Water
- Non-corrosive stirring tool
- Gloves
- Salt
- Urea

Safety

Work outside, or in a well-ventilated area. Wear gloves, a respirator, and eye protection. Avoid prolonged exposure to bleach fumes and neutralizer powder. Do not smoke, eat, or drink around bleach or while working with discharging.

Keep bleach, neutralizer, and prepared baths away from pets and children.

Do not dispose of bleach and neutralizer solution where it can contaminate pets, plants, children, food, or eating utensils. For the relatively small amount of chemicals used with occasional discharging, it is safe to dispose of baths in household drains as long as you allow the water to run for several minutes to dilute the bleach.

5   Different dyes and fabrics show different results, which may not be what you expect. A strip of untreated rust-orange hand-dyed cotton is shown on the left. The right strip shows the results of dipping the fabric in the bleach bath for about ten seconds, which created a golden yellow color.

6   For an allover effect, submerge the fabric in the bleach bath and gently agitate it to make sure the bleach is absorbed evenly.

7   For a color block or patterned effect, dip selected areas of fabric in the bleach.

8   The longer the bleach is on the fabric, the more color will be removed. However, if bleach is left on the fabric for too long, it will damage the fibers. Therefore, when the desired shade is reached, quickly and carefully remove the fabric and put it in the rinse bath. Stir gently to remove excess bleach, then place the fabric in the neutralizer bath. Follow manufacturer instructions for soaking time. While the fabric is soaking in the neutralizer solution, dump out the rinse water and refill the rinse container with clean water. Once the bleach is neutralized, move the fabric to the clean rinse bath. Rinse thoroughly, then wash using textile detergent.

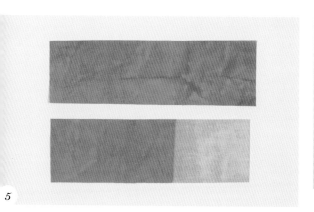

5

7

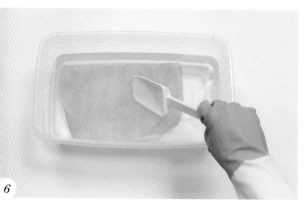

6

8

TIE-DYEING

1 It's easier to manipulate dry fabric, so fold your fabric first. To create a pattern, fold fabric along one edge, then fold it back on itself, accordion-style. With the long edge facing you, fold a triangle of the fabric, then fold the triangle back on itself. Continue down the length of the fabric until you have a thick fabric triangle. Secure the folded fabric with rubber bands.

2 Soak fabric in dye activator solution for fifteen minutes. Press lightly on the fabric to help the solution penetrate through the folded layers.

3 While the fabric is soaking, prepare your dye solution. (See the Tie-Dyeing chart on page 165.) You'll need about ½ cup (120 ml) of each color that you plan to use. Mix the dye solution and pour it into squeeze bottles.

TOOLS AND MATERIALS

- Plant-based (cellulose) fabric, such as cotton, linen, rayon, etc. Silk fabric will also work.
- Rubber bands
- Non-corrosive stirring tool
- Measuring spoon
- Procion MX dyes
- Plastic measuring cup with pour spout
- Squeeze bottle(s)
- Shallow plastic container
- Chemical solutions: urea water and dye activator solution
- Shallow plastic container
- Textile detergent

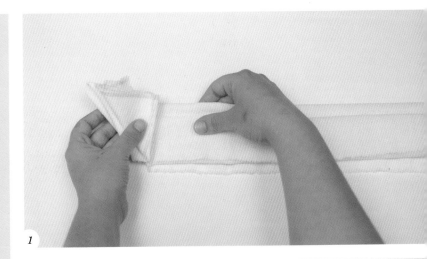

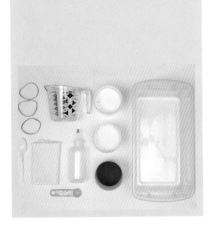

1

2

Hints and tips

If you want to layer different colors, it's helpful to keep the color wheel in mind as a general guide to matching colors.

4 Now for the fun part! Starting with the lightest color, apply dye solution to the fabric. Go slowly and let the fabric absorb the dye solution before adding more dye.

5 Apply the next color, and again allow the fabric to absorb the solution as you work. Keep working in this manner until all colors are applied.

6 Batch the fabric according to the instructions on pages 70–71. This allows the chemical reaction to exhaust itself. Once batching is finished, remove the fabric from the batching container, remove the rubber bands, unfold the fabric, and admire your results. Fill a container with cool water and rinse thoroughly. Wash in textile detergent according to manufacturer instructions, then dry and press as desired.

4

6

5

SHIBORI
Sewn-and-gathered and pole-wrapped resists

1   To create a sewn-and-gathered pattern, sew a long running stitch from one end of the fabric to the other. This can be done by hand, but you can also use a sewing machine set to the longest stitch length. Mark straight lines on the fabric as guides, or feel free to experiment.

2   Gather fabric along the sewing by pulling the fabric along the thread. You can keep the piece flat and secure the gathering by knotting the thread at either end, or you can make a fabric tube by knotting one end of the thread to the other, as shown below. If you've used a sewing machine, gather the fabric by pulling the bobbin threads and knot the top thread to the bottom thread on either side of the fabric.

3   To create a pole-wrapped pattern, wind a strip of fabric around a pipe. Work with long, narrow strips, or you may want to experiment with folding wider pieces. Hold the fabric at an angle at the bottom of the pipe and, in the same hand, hold your string. Begin to wind the fabric around the pipe, overlapping slightly as you go. Once you've covered about one half to three-quarters of the pipe, begin to wrap the string over the fabric, again on an angle.

TOOLS AND MATERIALS

- Plant-based (cellulose) fabric such as cotton, linen, rayon, etc. Silk fabric will also work with this technique
- Needle
- Thread
- Non-corrosive pipe section Note: PVC pipes found in hardware/plumbing supply stores work well
- String

- Dyebath container
- Procion MX dyes
- Salt
- Urea
- Dye activator
- Medium plastic container (6–12 qt/5.6–11.3 l)
- Non-corrosive stirring tool
- Measuring spoon
- Mixing cup
- Textile detergent

PVC piping comes in a variety of thicknesses and diameters, and the length can be cut to order in the hardware store. It's a good idea to keep a range of sizes for use with different projects.

4 Once you have a section of fabric and string wrapped, scrunch the fabric and string down to the end of the pole. Continue wrapping and scrunching fabric and string until all the fabric is wrapped and scrunched. Wrap the end of the string around the top edge of the fabric and knot to secure it.

5 Decide on the color and saturation that you want to dye your fabric. Prepare your dyebath according to the instructions on pages 74–75.

6 Place bound/prepared fabric in the dyebath container and pour the dye over the fabric. You can really experiment here with different values of the same fabric or even layering different colors. Let the fabric sit in the dyebath for thirty to forty-five minutes. It's best not to agitate the fabric or press on it—you don't want to hide the work you did to pattern the fabric. Remove the fabric from the dyebath and rinse. Pull out the sewing and unwrap the fabric from the pipe. Rinse again until the fabric feels clean, the dye may still run from the fabric. Wash it in textile detergent, then dry and press as desired.

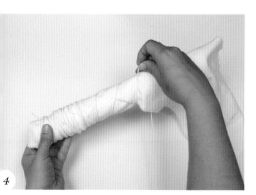

4

6

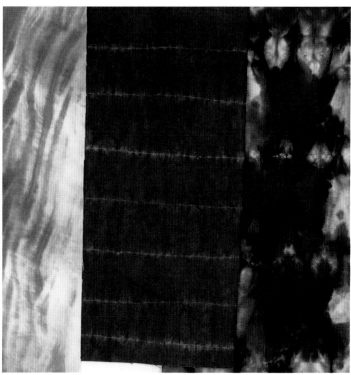

SOY WAX BATIK

1 Melt the soy wax over your heat source according to manufacturer instructions. While the wax is melting, mark your design on the fabric. You will need to work quickly, so it's best to keep your design simple. Once the wax has melted, place your brush in the wax to allow it to come up to temperature.

2 Apply the wax to the fabric. You'll have to work fairly quickly and spontaneously because the wax needs to be applied while it is hot.

3 For best results, check the back of your fabric to make sure the wax is penetrating the fibers.

4 Once the design is waxed, prepare the dyebath (see pages 74–75). Because of the heat involved, natural dyes are not recommended for this process. Now you are ready to dye!

TOOLS AND MATERIALS

- Soy wax
- Heat source (for melting the wax)
- Natural bristle brush. Note: the heat involved in this process may melt synthetic bristles
- Plant-based (cellulose) fabric, such as cotton, linen, rayon, etc.
- Dyebath
- Procion MX dyes
- Salt
- Urea
- Dye activator
- Measuring spoon
- Non-corrosive stirring tool
- Medium plastic container (12 qt/11.3 l)
- Mixing cups

1

2

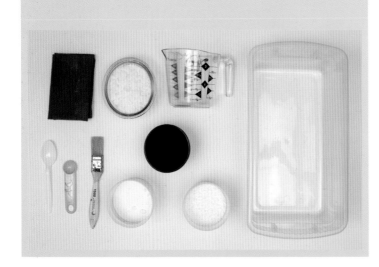

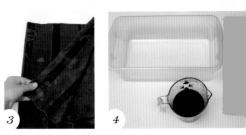

3

4

Hints and tips

Use an enclosed heat source to melt the wax. Wax is flammable, so do not melt the wax using an open flame. Be sure your wax container can tolerate the heat and does not leak. A pancake griddle and a clean tin can are ideal.

This tutorial focuses on soy wax because it is less toxic and is easier to remove than petroleum-based waxes.

5 Thoroughly wet the fabric and submerge it in the dyebath. Allow it to sit in the dyebath for thirty minutes. Occasional gentle agitation will give a more even color, but too much agitation may flake the wax off the fabric.

6 Once the fabric is dyed, discard the dye solution, fill the plastic container with clean water, and agitate gently to rinse the fabric. Discard the rinse water and repeat until the fabric feels clean. To remove the wax, wash in hot water with textile detergent. Dry and press as desired.

7 You can also remove wax by pressing the fabric between layers of newsprint with an iron, although you may want to experiment to be sure that the wax doesn't penetrate the fabric and leave a waxy residue. If you've used a lot of wax, this is a good way to minimize the amount of wax you'll be washing out.

5

6

DIP DYEING AND OVER DYEING

1   Soak the fabric in the dye activator solution for fifteen minutes. Agitate gently to make sure that all of the fabric is saturated.

2   While the fabric is soaking, prepare your dye solution according to the Dip Dyeing and Over Dyeing chart on page 165. Measure your dye into your mixing container and add urea water to make one cup of dye activator solution. Pour the dye solution into the small plastic container you will be using to dye with.

3   Decide where you want the color on your fabric and manipulate the fabric so that you will be able to dip just that area into the dye.

TOOLS AND MATERIALS

- Plant-based (cellulose) fabric, such as cotton, linen, rayon, etc. Note: silk will also work with this technique
- Dye activator
- Non-corrosive stirring tool
- Measuring spoon
- Procion MX dyes
- Small plastic container (½–6 qt/0.4–5.6 l)
- Plastic cup for mixing
- Chemical solutions: urea water and dye activator solution
- Textile detergent

1

3

Hints and tips

If you're over dyeing patterned fabrics, consider value (the lightness of a fabric) and the amount of contrast you're hoping to achieve with your over dye. Try working with fabric that is either fairly light in value or has a great deal of contrast in the pattern.

If you're working with solid fabrics, you'll likely achieve the best result with 100 percent cotton fabrics.

4 Let the fabric soak in the dyebath for thirty minutes. Remove the fabric and allow the excess dye solution to drip back into the dyebath container. Remove the fabric from the small plastic dyeing container, drain any residual dye solution, and replace the fabric. You will use the same container you used for dyeing for batching. Now batch the fabric following the instructions on page 70–71.

5 Once batching has been completed, remove the fabric from the container and rinse it with cool water until fabric feels clean, even though dye may still be running from the fabric. Wash in textile detergent, following manufacturer instructions. Dry and press as desired.

4

5

DYEING AND BLEACHING

Gallery

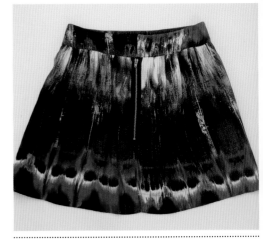

Tie-dyed skirt. By Anoushka Alden

Striped fabric. Handpainted and sun-printed using textile paints and tape. By Deborah O'Hare

Handpainted silk wrapped around a wooden bracelet and fixed with colored copper wire.
By Egle Minkuviene

Lily Kimono chiffon wrap, handpainted with resist technique. By Takuyo Williams

Spring Bloom silk chiffon scarf, handpainted with resist technique. By Takuyo Williams

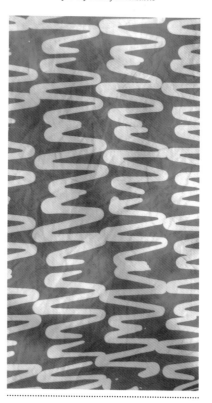

Hand-dyed wax resist using an onion cutter.
By Fabienne Chabrolin

Streams of Water. Fiber art created from hand-dyed and commercial cotton and silk fibers, hand- and machine-pieced, appliquéd, sewn, and embellished. By Lorie McCown

Encroachment. Fiber art created from hand-dyed cotton, silk fabric, and fibers. Hand- and machine-appliquéd, sewn, and quilted. By Lorie McCown

Smocked handbag made from batiked linen with leather details. By Estella Straatsma

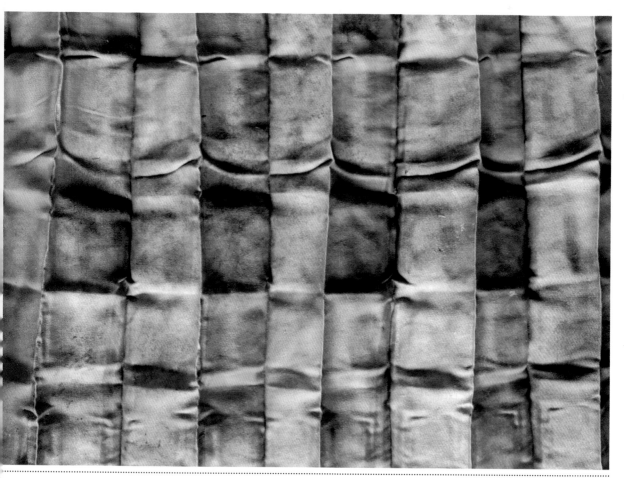

Silk fabric dyed with a technique called hapa-zome, where leaves and petals are placed between two pieces of fabric and a hammer used to transfer the natural botanical dyes directly to the fabric. By Marchi Wierson

SARA
HOPP

Interview

Sara Hopp earned her MFA in Printmaking from Louisiana State University, following a BFA from Syracuse University. She currently lives in Baton Rouge, Louisiana, where she creates her collections of textile art and home goods.

www.fiveoclockcrows.com

Can you describe your studio/ work space?

I have one worktable in my kitchen for dyeing. A sewing machine and clean worktable are located in a spare room along with books, sketches, and objects of inspiration.

Please describe your work and the materials you generally use.

Working with natural fibers, my process typically starts with hand-dyeing. I may work very directly, patterning fabric to make functional pieces such as scarves, napkins, or tea towels. I might also meander, looking at different fabrics and bringing them together in a quilt top or responding to a sketch to create an art piece.

Do you consider yourself a generalist or a specialist?

I'm a specialist because of my use of dyeing and resist processes, but within that niche I could be considered a generalist since my finished product can be a bed quilt, table linen, art quilt, or even sculpture.

Alternate cotton sateen throw quilt.

Pause pattern batik linen tea towel.

Batik linen tea towels.

In addition to dyeing/resists, what other creative pursuits do you practice?
I enjoy printmaking, photography, and baking.

Where do you find inspiration?
I find most inspiration from nature, historical patterns, and fine art.

How do you market your art?
I have my own website, blog, and online shop. I involve myself in the local arts scene, participating in and attending markets and events in order to meet other artisans as well as connect with new and existing customers.

"I find most inspiration from nature, historical patterns, and fine art."

Do you have advice for someone who wants to try dyeing/resists?
Starter kits are great introductions. Experiment, keep an open mind, and enjoy the process. Be confident and persistent and don't be afraid of failure. Every failure is a learning opportunity.

Are there any new techniques you'd like to try?
I'd really like to experiment with silk-screening resists onto fabric.

What do you see next for you and your career?
I hope to expand my pattern range and experiment with combining printing and dyeing processes.

Is there a design you're most proud of?
I really enjoy my Chevalet pattern because of the balance between positive and negative space it achieves. I'm also proud of my Candy Apple color. It took a lot of trial and error to create that perfect red.

"I involve myself in the local arts scene, participating in and attending markets and events in order to meet other artisans as well as connect with new and existing customers."

Chevalet pattern batik cotton/linen blend napkins.

Cotton throw pillow patterned with gathered machine-stitched shibori.

5 EMBELLISHMENT

by Megan Van Sipe

Choosing a fabric that you love is the best way to begin! Once
you've selected your fabrics, start to brainstorm and experiment
with which embellishments will work well with that specific fabric
type and design. The majority of the techniques in this chapter
work best on fabrics that are easy to sew through, but are also sturdy
enough to support additional elements with a bit of weight to them.
Consider light- to medium-weight cottons and wools, or similar.

Embellishment is all about adding something extra-special
to your fabric:

- Use sequins, studs, or beads to create shine and add detail
  to existing patterns.

- Play with adding lace, fringe, or ribbons for softer design elements.

- Take objects that are usually functional, like buttons and zippers,
  and see how you can use them visually instead of practically.

- Think three-dimensionally with your design and sculpt felt
  into textural art.

- Create your own details within your fabric by drawing them
  in with thread.

You can also consider how using different embellishments
on your fabric may help to evoke a certain feeling. Use them to
make it personal and more special. Try combining techniques
that inspire you. Think about how the different textures will add
interest and personality to the piece. You can have a lot of fun
sourcing embellishments as well. There are huge varieties of
vintage buttons, exotic beads, shapes and sizes of studs—
and more—that can make your project completely yours.

I urge you to get inspired by these techniques and then
push them further. Make your fabrics extraordinary!

SEQUINS

1 To create a layered, fish-scale technique, determine where the bottom of your design will be and begin by placing the first sequin at the bottom edge of your fabric.

2 Thread the beading needle and secure the sequin to the fabric by coming up through the middle of the sequin and then stitching down at the top. The top half of your sequin will be secure but the bottom half will be left unattached.

3 Stitch more sequins down in the same way, one directly next to the other, across the bottom of your design. Repeat the process with the next row, but layer this row over the first row, staggered, as shown.

TOOLS AND MATERIALS

- Fabric
- Sequins
- Thread
- Beading needle
- Scissors
- Seed beads (optional)

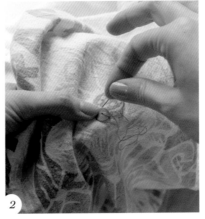

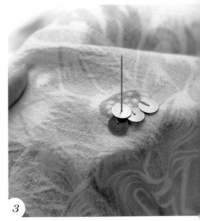

Hints and tips

Choose a fabric with design elements that can be filled in; this will give you a ready-made layout on which to place your sequins.

Flat sequins are easy to work with, but you can also use traditional faceted sequins with the techniques described in this tutorial.

Using a beading needle makes it easier to attach sequins that have tiny holes in their centers

 4 As an additional embellishment, you can also use small seed beads to secure the sequins. Come up through the back of the fabric and through the sequin, adding a bead to the needle. Once you've pulled the thread all the way through, move the bead slightly to the side so you can go back down through the hole of the sequin without going through the hole of the bead. The bead will keep the sequin in place.

 5 As an alternative method to the fish-scale pattern, you can stitch the sequins flat to the fabric using a varied number of stitches. Using contrasting thread or varying your stitch placement can also add additional pattern to your work. The more stitches you use, the more secure the sequins will be.

BEADING

1   Following the existing lines created in the fabric pattern, use seed beads to trace the edge and create a more defined shape for your design. Due to their small size, seed beads are a great choice for detail work.

2   By using beads which are complementary to the shapes/lines you'll be creating, you can enhance the fabric pattern with newly-imagined details. The beads used here are rectangle-shaped bugle beads.

TOOLS AND MATERIALS
- Patterned fabric
- Beads (seed beads, bugle beads, additional beads of choice)
- Beading needle
- Thread
- Scissors

1

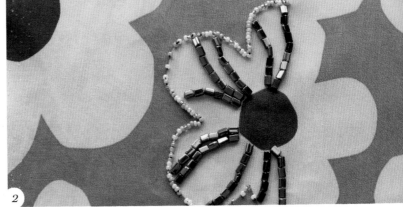

2

Hints and tips

To create a varied texture within your design, select a variety of bead sizes, materials, and types.

Alternatively, using a single type of bead can be impactful when you emphasize the layout pattern of the beads you choose.

Think carefully about your fabric choice. The placement of your beads should be incorporated so that they complement or add to the design and don't end up visually competing with it. Leaving empty space within your design can help draw the eye to the beaded portion of your work.

3 A great way to create a focal point within the design is with a unique, stand-out bead.

4 Using beads to fill in spaces within your fabric pattern creates lines and adds texture and interest. Here, the rest of the flower center has been filled with complementary-colored seed beads to accentuate the focal point.

3

4

ZIPPERS

1 Plan out the placement of your zipper with the zipper open at the top and the teeth facing toward the edges of the fabric. The edge of your fabric could be a neckline, hem, armhole, or even the edge of fabric yardage. Let the base of the zipper dip down into your fabric and then open up once it gets to the edge.

2 Determine where on your fabric you'd like the zipper to end. Using your fabric marker, mark your fabric at the zipper end. This will be your guide to show you how far down the fabric to cut.

3 Cut almost all the way down your drawn line, stopping ¼" (6 mm) from the mark you made. Make two small ¼" (6 mm) slices diagonally to the left and right of the mark. This will allow you to fold this fabric under when you sew in the zipper base.

TOOLS AND MATERIALS
- Metal-toothed zipper
- Fabric
- Fabric marker
- Scissors
- Sewing pins
- Needle and thread (or sewing machine)

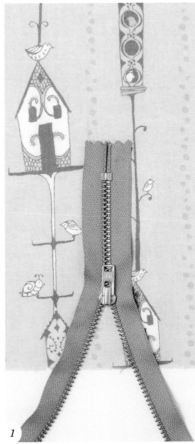

1

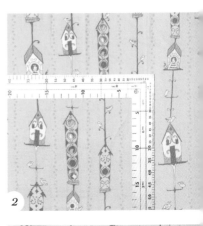

2

3

Hints and tips

Use zippers to create new lines within your fabrics. Adding them to a simple jersey t-shirt, cotton skirt, or other item from your closet will give it a more industrial feel. Try curving, folding, or even layering zippers for different effects.

For the most decorative impact, choose coat zippers or vintage zippers with big metal teeth.

Use fabrics that are sturdy enough to support the weight of your zipper.

Be creative with your stitches—this zipper doesn't have to be functional, it's embellishment!

4 Pin the zipper, beginning at the base (tucking the raw edges of the fabric under), and align the zip teeth with the edge of the fabric.

5 Starting at the base, attach the zipper to your fabric along the edge of the zipper. This stitching is meant to be decorative, so use any stitch you like. You can also consider using a contrasting thread.

6 A second row of stitching is not always necessary, but it can help to support the weight of the zipper and prevent it from turning outward.

7 Curving the zipper sharp at the corners as it turns onto the edges of your fabric gives a really modern and customized look. Hide the ends of your zipper on the inside of your fabric and stitch them down to finish.

4

6

5

7

FRINGE

1 To begin creating your own fringe from a non-woven fabric, cut a strip that is long enough for your project and as tall as you'd like the fringe to be. The fabric used here is wool felt.

2 With small fabric scissors, carefully create vertical cuts along your strip of fabric, stopping approximately ¼" (6 mm) from the edge. If your fringe is longer than the example, you can leave more than ¼" (6 mm) at the top to have a bigger area to attach the fringe if necessary.

3 Pin your fringe in place across the fabric at the lowest point. When layering fringe, you should start at the bottom and work your way up the fabric in order to make sewing easier.

4 After securing your first layer of fringe with a line of stitching, prepare the next row. To create a very tightly layered look, pin the next layer of fringe to the fabric just above the first layer.

TOOLS AND MATERIALS

- Assorted fringe
- Non-woven fabric
  (for handmade fringe, optional)
- Small fabric scissors
- Sewing pins
- Fabric
- Needle and thread
  (or sewing machine)

1

3

2

4

Hints and tips

Recommended fabrics for creating your own fringe include wool felt, leather, faux-leather, or suede. Any material that doesn't have much stretch or doesn't fray will work.

Using multiple colors of one type of fringe, or multiple types of fringe in one project, can be fun and challenging. Explore your fringe options and think outside the box.

Aside from sewing the fringe directly across fabric, consider inserting it into seams or along hems, borders, or necklines as well.

5 To get a great color impact and create a striped effect, plan the rest of your fringe layout. Mix a few types of fringe to give your project a quirky, off-beat feel. Think about the textures of your fringe and layer appropriately. Fringe that will lay flat looks best at the bottom, for example.

6 Continue to pin and sew the layers of fringe down close together, as shown in Step 4. The tightly placed fringe creates a different texture from what you would get if it were well spaced apart.

5

6

STUDS

1   Using the existing pattern on your fabric is a great way to design the layout for your studs. To easily remember your planned layout, lay the studs in place and snap a quick photo that you can refer to as you work.

2   To attach studs with prongs, hold the fabric securely in one hand and push the prongs carefully through the fabric. If using a woven or knit fabric, gently twisting the stud back and forth slightly as you push through the fabric often helps guide the fibers away from the prongs.

3   Flip the fabric over carefully while holding the stud in place so that it doesn't fall back out. Make sure your prongs are all the way through and give the fabric a little tug near each prong to make sure.

4   Continue to securely hold the stud and fabric with one hand. Then take your teaspoon in the other hand and firmly press the prongs inward, one at a time. Depending on the stud, it might take a bit of strength to get the bending started.

TOOLS AND MATERIALS

- Studs
- Patterned fabric
- Small scissors or an awl tool (both optional)
- Metal teaspoon

1

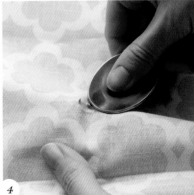

3

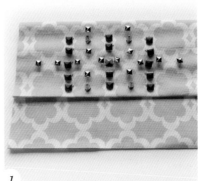

2

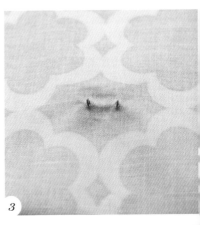

4

Hints and tips

Very thin fabrics, such as chiffon, are not a good choice for studs because they don't hold up to the weight very well. Use fabrics that are at least as thick as quilting cotton or thicker.

Choosing a variety of studs is a great way to play with creating patterns within your stud layout.

To help guide you in creating an interesting layout, choose a fabric with a geometric print.

If you use leather or fabric of similar texture, an awl tool will help you considerably by creating holes in the fabric before pushing the stud through.

5 It is sometimes good to give the prongs a second push inward, just to be sure they're secure. It's best if the prongs are pointing down and inward a bit, so they don't snag on anything later.

6 If you have a stud that has a screw-in back instead of prongs, poke a small hole in your fabric before pushing the stud through. For woven or knit fabric, small scissors will work well for this. If using leather or similarly thick fabric, an awl is a better choice for puncturing a clean hole through your material.

7 Push the back piece of the stud upward through the hole you created. The hole should be just big enough that the stud does not have to stretch the fabric in order to fit through.

8 Holding the back of the stud in place with one hand, screw on the top part of the stud until it tightens all the way.

9 The stud should lay flat against the fabric and completely cover the hole that you created.

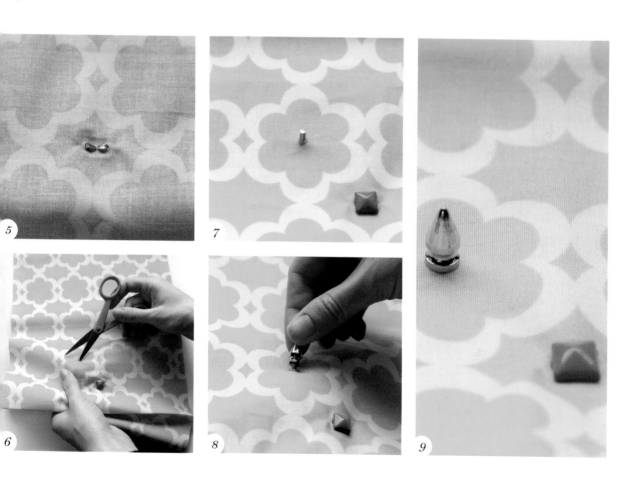

5

6

7

8

9

LACE

1   Cut your fabric to the appropriate size for your project and create a layout for your lace pieces. Think about the placement in terms of creating a motif, border, or focal point.

2   To insert lace across a border or hem, cut straight across the fabric and separate the two pieces, making room for the lace between them.

3   You want to be able to see through the lace without there being any fabric behind it, so carefully place the top edge of your lace along the cut edge of your fabric. Overlap the two just enough so that you will be able to secure it down with thread. Use small stitches and inconspicuously stitch the lace down to the fabric.

4   Using the same method, stitch the remaining piece of your fabric to the bottom edge of the lace.

TOOLS AND MATERIALS
- Fabric
- Lace
- Thread
- Scissors

1

3

2

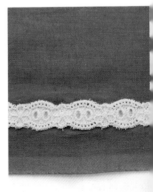

4

Hints and tips

Choose a thread color that closely matches your lace so that your stitching will be invisible.

Lace can get lost in a fabric that is too busy, so choose a simple fabric print or solid fabric with this technique.

5 Be sure the fabric lays nice and flat so that you don't have any shifting or puckering once you're finished stitching.

6 It can be a nice touch to create an area in the lace where you can see through to the fabric underneath. To do this, stitch with small, close stitches around the area that you'd like to see through. In this example, I chose the center circle of this lace motif.

7 Check your stitches to make sure they are flat.

8 In order to create a window out of the lace, you'll need to remove the fabric from the center circle. From the back of the fabric, slowly and very carefully cut away the fabric close to your stitching edge, so you do not accidentally snip any part of the lace on the other side.

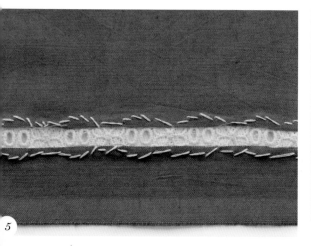

5

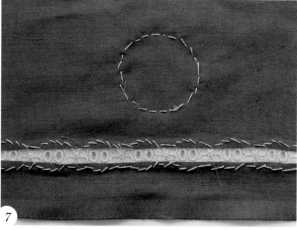

7

6

8

RIBBONS

Technique 1: Diamond Pleating

1 Sew straight down the middle of your ribbon to keep it secure. For best results, use a thread that matches your ribbon color.

2 Using pins, mark spots that are evenly spaced across your ribbon. For a wide ribbon, mark every 4" (10 cm) or so. If your ribbon is smaller, you can decrease the spacing.

3 Remove alternating pins and sew vertically down the ribbon. Every other pin remains in place to mark where we will be folding.

4 Where the pins remain, bring the top and bottom edges of the ribbon inward to meet at the center stitching and pin to secure.

5 While maintaining the folds, carefully remove the pins and sew vertically down the ribbon to secure your newly formed pleats. You can leave the ribbon looking three-dimensional or you can iron flat as shown.

TOOLS AND MATERIALS
- Sewing machine
- Assorted ribbons
- Sewing pins
- Scissors
- Fabric
- Iron (optional)

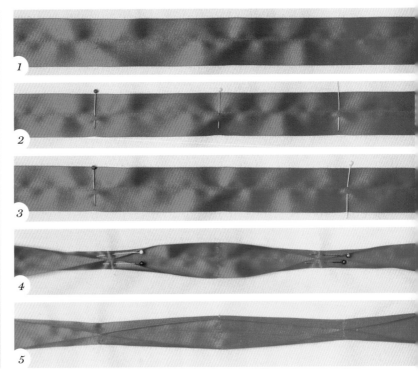

Hints and tips

Using ribbons of various types will give you more room to play with different techniques. Velvet, wire-edged, thick grosgrain, jacquard, and double-sided are all great options.

Technique 2: Box Pleating

1 To create a box pleat, fold two pleats inward toward each other, leaving a bit of space in between. Repeat this technique with the spacing you prefer and experiment for a different look.

2 Sew directly down the center all along the ribbon to secure the pleats. Leaving the edges free gives the pleating more texture.

Technique 3: Zigzag Folding

1 For a double-sided ribbon, play with showing off both sides by using a zigzag fold. Pin the beginning of your ribbon down to keep it flat, then fold the ribbon down at a 45-degree angle and pin. Fold the ribbon back up at an angle and pin again.

2 Zigzag the ribbon haphazardly, pinning at each fold. Have fun and play with folding—it's not meant to be perfect!

3 Stitch down the center, following your zigzag as much as you can. You could stitch this down along the top and bottom edges, or secure it down the middle only on one side of the ribbon and leave the other loose.

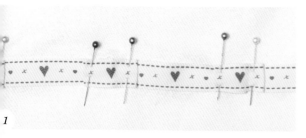

1

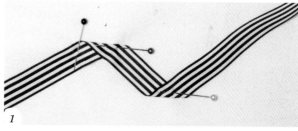

1

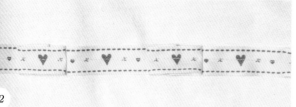

2

2

3

3

RIBBONS

Technique 4: Pleating

1 Pleating a ribbon with wire edges allows for the ultimate textural pleat. Fold even pleats all in the same direction and pin.

2 Stitch down the center along the ribbon to secure pleats, then lift and rough up the pleats a bit to allow the wire to give the pleats more volume.

Technique 5: Ruffling

1 A simple way to ruffle a ribbon is to scrunch up one end just a bit by hand, then pin it. You can also scrunch and create the ruffles as you feed the ribbon and fabric through a sewing machine. Keep your stitching along the top edge of the ribbon for the best ruffle effect.

2 Manually gathering your ribbon to create ruffles allows for maximum control over how much volume you create as you sew. Loose and imperfect ruffling looks romantic and not too contrived.

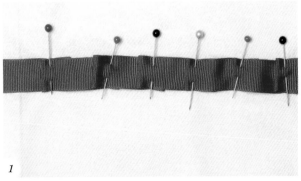

1

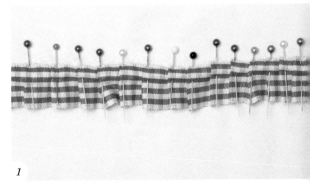

1

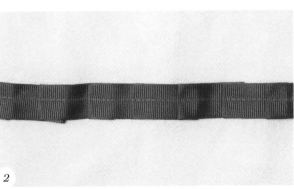

2

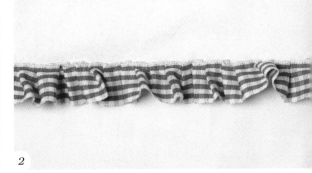

2

Hints and tips

For folding, pleating, and ruffling techniques, wider ribbons are the best choice.

Use a ruler if you would like to create perfectly even pleats.

Technique 6: Pleated Flower

1 A pleated flower is another fun way to use ribbon to add personality to a project. Using regular, loose pleats, fold and pin in a circle, leaving room in the center for more rows. To begin, only pin your first row until you are close to meeting back where you began.

2 Sew along the bottom edge of the pleats, carefully removing the pins one by one as you go. The pleats should now look loose and ruffled.

3 Begin pinning your next row of pleats in the same manner as the first row. Make sure you're decreasing the size of your center circle so you can see the previous layer of pleats easily along the outer edge.

4 Sew around the inner edge as you did before, leaving you with two pretty rows of pleats and just a small center circle to fill.

5 Without pins this time, carefully fold and sew your ribbon until you work your way to the center. Tuck your edge under and stitch down to secure at the very center of your flower.

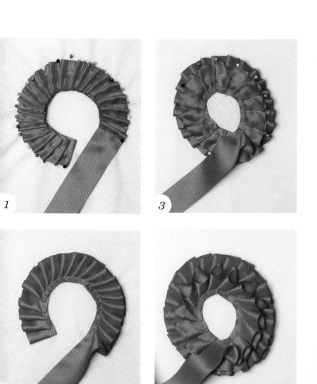

BUTTONS

1. Determine where you will be attaching your buttons, using their width as a guide, and start marking the fabric. (It can be easier not to mark if you're stitching your buttons close together.)

2. With a knot at the end of your thread, attach the button by starting from the back of the fabric.

3. Instead of the traditional button-stitching technique, stitch back down near the outside edge of the button.

4. Come up through the next button hole and reflect what you've done in the previous step.

TOOLS AND MATERIALS
- Buttons
- Fabric
- Marker (optional)
- Scissors
- Sewing needle
- Thread

1

2

3

4

Hints and tips

Choose thread that matches the buttons in order to let the buttons stand out in the design. Alternatively, choose a contrasting thread to highlight the unique stitching technique used.

5 You can end here, or continue to play with the number of stitches coming from the button holes. Be sure to stitch in various directions.

6 Continue attaching buttons in a similar manner. You can experiment with the direction and number of stitches if you would like to add some variation to your project.

7 Clustering buttons close together and stitching them in varying patterns adds more interest and texture.

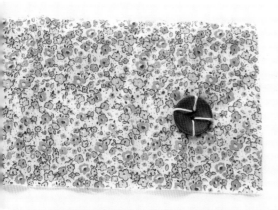

5

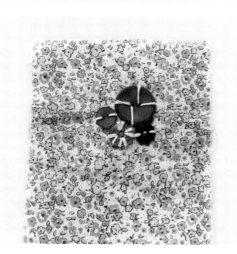

6

7

FELT

1 Cut felt into squares of the following sizes: 4" (10 cm) squares (cut eleven), 3" (7.5 cm) squares (cut nine). Keep the two piles separate. Cut one 5" (12.5 cm) circle.

2 Cut the squares into the petal shape of your choice, leaving the bottom of the petal flat. Think of the texture you want your flower to have when deciding on your petal shape. Rounded, ruffled, sharp, symmetrical, organic—a variety of different looks can be achieved with a slight variation.

3 Secure the 5" (12.5 cm) circle to your fabric with a simple running stitch. This will act as the base for your flower petals.

4 Starting with the large petals, stitch them down to the flower base following the edge as a guide. Ruffle, bend, and pleat the petal base as you stitch down, to give it movement and texture.

TOOLS AND MATERIALS

- Fabric scissors
- Felt
- Ruler
- Fabric
- Embroidery needle
- Embroidery floss
- Rotary cutter and mat (optional)
- Embellishments of your choice

1

3

2

4

Hints and tips

A wool-blend felt works much better than its synthetic counterpart in terms of cutting ease and hand-feel.

Cut one petal and use it as a template, or cut each freehand for an organic look.

You may need more or fewer petals depending on how closely together you stitch them.

5 With the small petals, begin the second row. Be sure to overlap, so that about half of this petal is laying on top of the previous row.

6 After stitching the second row of petals, only about 2" (5 cm) of the base should be showing in the center. Fluff your petals up to give your flower some volume.

7 Add a dramatic center using your choice of embellishment: fringe, buttons, sequins, ribbon—anything exciting that will give more texture and personality to the flower.

EMBELLISHMENT
Gallery

Clutch appliquéd with vintage hand-crocheted doily. By Tuija Lommi

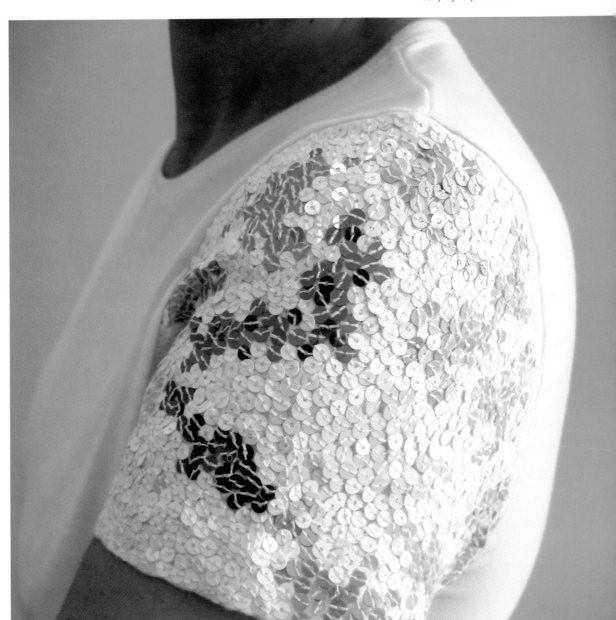

Plain white, cotton T-shirt embroidered with different colored sequins. By Stella Padão

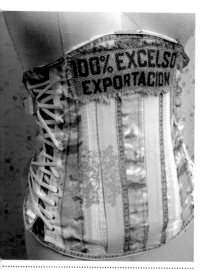

Excelsor Corset. Burlap coffee bag appliqué and textile ribbon trim on vintage corset. By Lori Sandstedt

Purse embellished with vintage lace doily. By Tuija Lommi

Mail organizer envelope featuring vintage cotton fabrics and freehand machine embroidery. By Tuija Lommi

Dress embellished with antique cotton crochet and textured yarn. By Carolyn Elliott, GEOLOGY urban fossil

Storytelling. Wall-hung quilt with machine embroidery and handstitching, photo transfer, acid etching, handpainting, and appliqué. Incorporates vintage ticking, silk, cotton, found objects, walnut ink, and buttons. By Kate Crossley. Photo by Keith Barnes

Necessary Comforts. Embroidered mini quilt with vintage floss, buttons, and heavy interfacing. By Victoria Gertenbach

Button belt. Wide elastic sewn with a mix of old buttons. By Kirsti Michelle of Makenzi & Madilyn Designs

Song of Solitude. Fabric collage using variety of fabric scraps and embellished with images transferred to fabric. By Laurie Dorrell

Frog Prince and Turtle Man. Pillow embellished with seed beads, faux pearls, and glass beads. Fabric is from Oceanica Panel from In the Beginning and was designed by illustrator Julie Paschkis. Beading and photos by Karen Lideen

Hunting Season. Embroidery on painted vintage leadshot sack embellished with floss, vintage hanger, text, and buttons. By Victoria Gertenbach

Old Ladies with Dogs. Drawn using sewing machine and applied onto patterned calico fabric. By Sarah Walton

MEGAN VAN SIPE

Interview

Lilac Saloon, Megan Van Sipes' studio, was born out of creative restlessness and her constant search for beauty. Megan's work combines texture with dimension through her designs and her favorite material to work with is felt. She works from a turquoise studio in Iowa, often with her cat Dahlia by her side.

lilacsaloon.com

Where are you located?

I live in a tiny, windy town in northern Iowa called Titonka. It's surrounded by corn and soybean fields for miles and miles! Our move to the middle of nowhere was essentially for my husband's career as a wind technician (working on those wind turbines in the middle of fields). You literally go where the wind takes you and as it so happens, they put wind turbines in the middle of nowhere almost always, so it was inevitable that we'd end up in a tiny town. Luckily for us, we love the quiet, friendly, slow-paced life.

Has living where you do changed what you work on?

It has allowed me to slow down and relax more, take things less seriously and live more sustainably. I live a less consumer lifestyle. It's easier to do when you're not bombarded by stores and convenience like you are in a bigger city. I think I am happier with life and that allows me to reflect those feelings and qualities into my work. Learning to use what we have and be less wasteful is part of our lifestyle here. That filtered into my work when I started making felt heart confetti out of the scraps leftover from creating Wallflowers. I focus on the small, beautiful details in my life and my work.

Name ornaments featuring sweet fabric prints and wool felt.

The white-on-white look is one of Megan's favorites because it allows you to really focus on the texture of the flowers without getting color involved.

A beautiful mess of felt heart confetti.

Are you formally trained as an artist/designer?

In college, I studied for a degree in apparel merchandising and design as well as business administration. After school, I worked in the fashion industry for a few years as a textile designer for Abercrombie & Fitch. Although the formal training in both of those areas has taught me a lot and brought diversity into my work, I have found that I like my work best when I just do what I want! So that's what I do.

Do you consider yourself a generalist or a specialist?

I haven't considered either! Maybe a creative explorer. I've never put myself into too much of a box. It leaves me open to growth and change.

"I have found that I like my work best when I just do what I want! So that's what I do."

Please describe your work and the materials you generally use.

I gravitate toward texture and color, and the more handcrafted the better. I'm obsessed with hand embroidery and love incorporating that into my work wherever I can. I also love working with wool felt to create floral art pieces because felt is so versatile for creating great textures. I like to experiment and have never really settled on creating one type of product. Manipulating fabric/felt and stitching by hand are my mainstays, though.

What other creative pursuits do you practice?

I love photography. I get really energized by photo shoots and dreaming up a whole concept. I love learning something challenging and photography can definitely be a challenge to pick up in the beginning. I began photography as an outlet that would feel different from making things as I normally do—but I've found it to be crucial to my business and can't imagine never having learned to use a good camera.

"I've never put myself into too much of a box when describing myself. It leaves me open to growth and change."

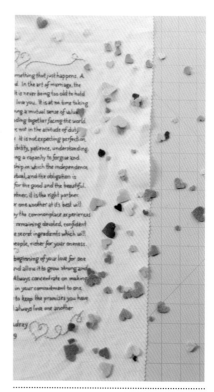

This hand-embroidered wedding vows keepsake took more than sixty hours of stitching to complete.

"When I am looking for more tangible inspiration, fashion is usually my first go-to source. Poring through fashion magazines and catching up on the runway shows usually gets my mind buzzing."

At just under 3" (7.5 cm), this sweet little flower hair clip is a mini version of Megan's popular Wallflowers.

Where do you find inspiration?

I love going for long walks with my camera, or also on mini road trips. Exploring old worn-down towns and imagining the history of the abandoned houses is my absolute favorite. I don't take literal inspiration from these experiences very often, but I find instead that I feel recharged and refreshed. Taking myself out of my normal environment is the best way to jump back into my work, inspired. When I am looking for more tangible inspiration, fashion is usually my first go-to source. Poring through fashion magazines and catching up on the runway shows usually gets my mind buzzing. Then I walk to the corn fields, just for good contrast.

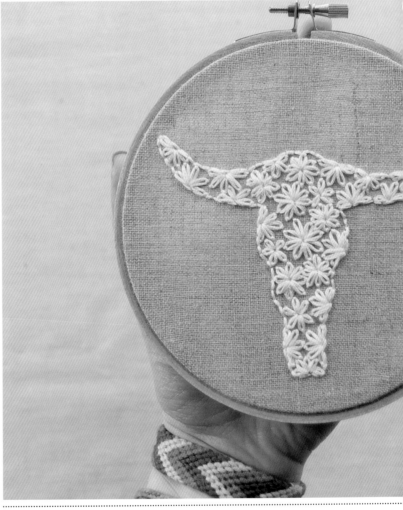

Big, bright, and dramatic Wallflowers bring life and texture to a room. They were inspired by Megan's favorite flower, the dahlia.

Megan's signature bull skull design with tiny flower-shaped embroidery stitches gives a feminine quality to an otherwise masculine shape.

How do you market your work?

I don't do much marketing. I've been allowing my business to grow organically without investing heavily into marketing sources that I couldn't be sure would be successful. I take strong, web-friendly photos so they're more likely to be featured on Etsy's front page and on blogs. I treat every customer as a friend and make sure they know that they're special and that I appreciate them. I am a perfectionist about the quality of my work. I rely heavily on word-of-mouth marketing.

Do you have advice for artists who are starting out regarding how to market and sell their work?

Beyond making a quality product that you are proud of and getting beautiful photographs of your work, I think connecting with your customers and networking with other creatives through blogging is a great (and free) way to get yourself out there. Share more about who you are. Let people know there is a real, cool person behind the work they are seeing. They'll love your work more once they love you!

Original embroidery design.

Are there any new techniques you'd like to try?

I would love to learn more about printing onto fabric. I spent the beginning of my career designing prints for fabric, but this was only computer-based. I never actually got to learn about physically printing onto the fabric. I'd love to experiment with this on a small scale to customize some of my wardrobe and maybe some home décor pieces as well. Combining that with a little embellishment would be right up my alley.

"I treat every customer as a friend and make sure they know that they're special."

Wallflower hanging ornament

Repurposed felt scraps turned into thousands of tiny felt hearts to be used as confetti.

6 SPECIALIST TECHNIQUES

by Rachel Hobson

One of the fastest, easiest, and least expensive ways to embellish your fabric is with needlework and appliqué. The techniques in this chapter are low effort, but high impact. You can transform cotton prints, create fresh, modern, and custom home décor, and even make stylish accessories with these skills and tools that have been in use for centuries.

First, you will learn how to transfer embroidery designs to your fabric. There are many ready-made designs available, or you can create your own pattern for a truly custom piece. Most transfer tools are very inexpensive and will last well into your embroidery adventures. We will begin our look at needlearts with the unique and exotic punchneedle embroidery. This rich and textural form of embroidery is a great way to turn a traditional art into a fresh, new medium.

Next, you will learn some very basic hand embroidery stitches that will work on just about any embroidery project you can imagine. Think of these as the foundation to your embroidery journey.

Where punchneedle offers rich texture and embroidery allows for a wide variety of stitches, cross-stitch creates crisp, precise designs.

Finally, we will explore the quick and easy art of appliqué. This is a fun way to work with prints and layer fabrics, creating great visual interest. Once you've appliquéd your fabric, you can further embellish it with any of the needlearts previously described in this chapter.

Most of these specialist techniques work best on linen, cotton, and evenweave fabrics. As you develop your skills, though, you can experiment on all kinds of textiles. While these projects focus on using six-stranded cotton embroidery floss, once you've gotten comfortable you can try working with pearl cotton floss, satin floss, and even ribbon and silk.

Start with simple projects to develop your own style and build your confidence. Above all, have fun and don't worry about perfection. The more fun you have with your stitchery, the more you will want to do it. The more you stitch, the better your stitching will get. Before you know it, you won't be able to look at fabric without thinking of some way to embellish it with needlework. Enjoy!

TRANSFERRING PATTERNS

Lightbox/window method

1 Tape the pattern you wish to transfer to the lightbox surface using painter's tape. Place the fabric on top of the pattern, and trace the design with a water-soluble or air-erasable marker.

2 If a lightbox is not available, tape your pattern to a sunny window. Tape or hold your fabric up over the pattern and trace the design with a water-soluble or air-erasable marker. After stitching your design, use a spray bottle to spritz away the markings, or wash the item by hand.

TOOLS AND MATERIALS
- Lightbox (if available)
- Painter's tape
- Fabric
- Water-soluble/air-erasable markers
- Needle and thread
- Spray bottle, filled with water
- Dressmaker's carbon transfer paper
- Stylus or ballpoint pen
- Iron (if using iron-on transfers)
- Iron-on transfer designs

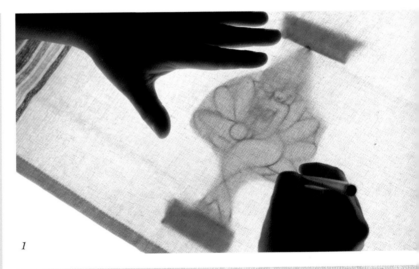

1

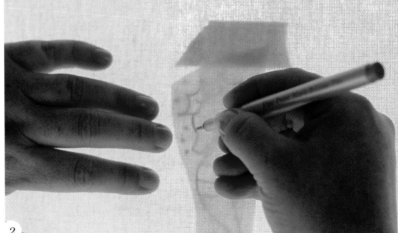

2

Hints and tips

When transferring a design onto light fabric, use a dark-colored transfer paper. When transferring a design onto dark-colored fabric, use a light-colored (white or yellow) transfer paper.

When using water-soluble and air-erasable markers, do not iron the markings or they will become permanently embedded in the fabric.

Dressmaker's carbon transfer paper can be found in the sewing notions section of your local craft or fabric store.

Dressmaker's carbon transfer paper method

1   Layer your materials down on a flat, hard surface in the following order: image to be transferred on top of carbon paper (dark side down), on top of the fabric.

2   Using a stylus or ballpoint pen, apply firm pressure and trace the design onto the fabric. Be careful not to shift the image while tracing.

1

2

TRANSFERRING PATTERNS

Iron-on method

1 Gather your materials and set your iron to high heat. Drain the water completely so you have a hot, dry iron with which to work. Press the base fabric to remove any wrinkles and to heat the fabric so the design transfers more easily.

2 Lay your image to be transferred face down on the fabric and press it with the hot, dry iron. If the design is larger than the iron, lift, move, and press to cover all of the design. Avoid sliding the iron back and forth to prevent the design from shifting on the fabric.

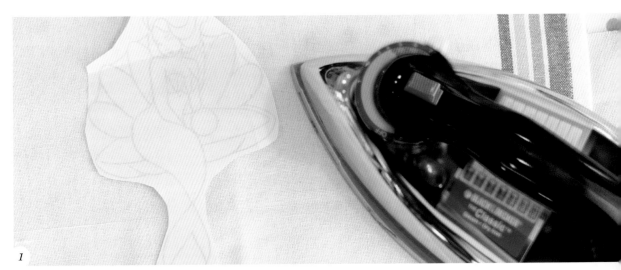

1

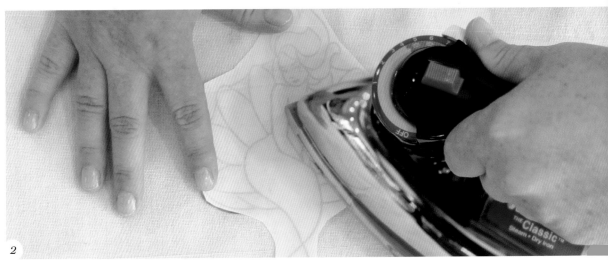

2

Hints and tips

Most iron-on transfer designs can be used several times. Impressions may be lighter with each use, but as long as you can see a faint line for stitching, the transfer can be used again and again.

3 Lift a small corner of the paper to see if the design has transferred to the fabric. Be very careful not to shift the design.

4 Remove the iron-on transfer carefully, as it will be very hot. Don't worry if your design has areas of light and dark transfer. As long as you can see a line, you can stitch the design.

3

4

PUNCHNEEDLE EMBROIDERY

1 Transfer your design to the back of the punchneedle fabric using your preferred method. Because you are transferring the image to the back side of the fabric, be sure to reverse any text so it reads correctly on the front.

2 Loosen the screw on the outer embroidery hoop and separate it from the inner hoop. Lay your fabric on top of the inner hoop with the design printed on the back of the fabric facing up. Open the outer hoop as wide as possible and push it down over the inner hoop. Tighten the screw on the hoop.

3 Separate your embroidery floss into three sections, each consisting of three strands. Hold the floss between your fingers and thumbs, and slide a fingernail into the floss to count out three strands.

4 Slide your thumbs into the floss and separate it, working out from the middle to avoid tangling. Set aside one set of the three strands of floss for later use.

TOOLS AND MATERIALS
- Needlepunch
- Needlepunch tool wire needle threader
- Cotton embroidery floss
- Needlepunch fabric or a cotton print
- Small embroidery scissors
- Embroidery hoop

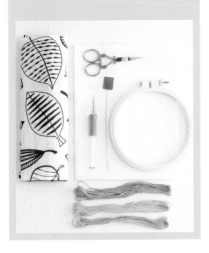

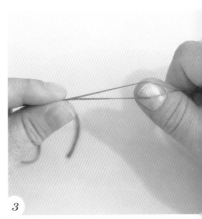

1

2

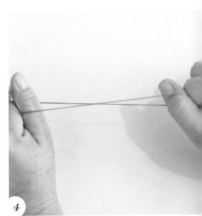

3

4

Hints and tips

Different punchneedle tools can accommodate different types and thicknesses of embroidery floss. Check your punchneedle tool's instructions for details.

Begin by punching the outline of the shape you are stitching and then go back to fill in.

5 To thread the punchneedle tool, take your thin wire needle threader and slide it through the needle end of the tool until it emerges from the bottom end.

6 Thread a small bit of the embroidery floss through the looped wire of the threader that is sticking out of the end of the punchneedle tool.

7 Pull the threader back through the tool, bringing the floss with it and out the needle end. Remove the floss from the wire threader..

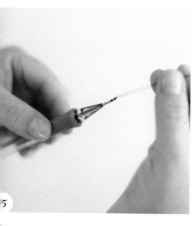

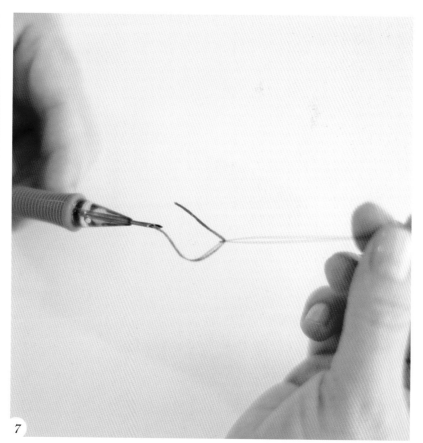

PUNCHNEEDLE EMBROIDERY

8 Insert the threader into the top side eye on the needle portion of the tool. Thread a couple of inches through the wire loop and pull it back through the eye of the needle. Remove the floss from the wire threader.

9 Pull the embroidery floss from the bottom of the tool until only about 1″ (2.5 cm) of floss remains protruding from the eye of the punchneedle tool.

10 Hold the punchneedle tool in your hand like a pencil and place it perpendicular to the fabric on the design line.

11 Push the punchneedle tool through the fabric until it hits the stopper on the tool.

8

10

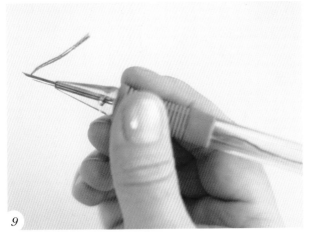

9

11

Hints and tips

As you stitch, do not be alarmed if areas of color seem to lack definition. As the design fills in completely, the loops will begin to stand up and become more defined.

Always punch with the beveled edge of the needle pointing into the next stitch. When you reach a turning point, either turn the needle completely and work in the next direction, or turn the hoop and stitch in the next direction.

12 Pull the tool back up until the needle point just exits the fabric. Lightly slide the needle across the fabric to the next stitch spot and press the punchneedle back into the fabric. Continue on around the border of the image and then go back to fill in.

13 When you reach the end of your thread, gently remove the needle and then snip the thread close to the base of the fabric. Threads should stay in place, but light fabric adhesive can be used to secure them if needed.

2

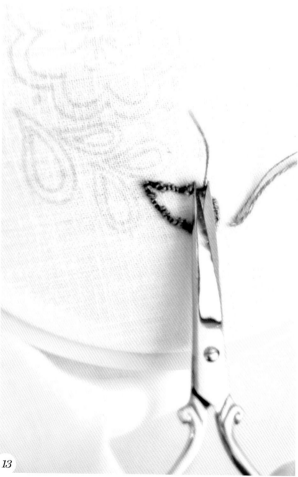

13

EMBROIDERY

1 Keeping in mind where the finished seams of your project will be, transfer your design to the fabric using one of the methods described on pages 124–127. In this example, I used a water soluble marker to write words on the fabric.

2 Cut a length of embroidery floss approximately 16" (40 cm) long and tie a simple knot in one end, clipping the tail close to the knot. Flatten the threads at the opposite end and thread about 2"–3" (5–7.5 cm) through the eye of your needle.

TOOLS AND MATERIALS

- Various cotton print fabrics
- Water soluble marker
- Cotton embroidery floss
- Small embroidery scissors
- Embroidery needle
- 4–6" (10–15 cm) embroidery hoop

1

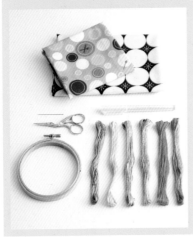

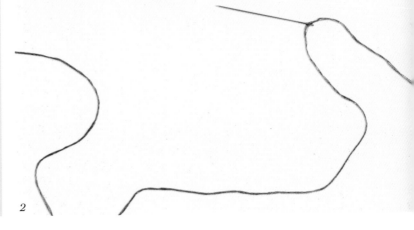

2

Hints and tips

Wash and dry all fabric before stitching. Fabric that is washed and dried after stitching may shrink and cause stitches to pucker.

Small embroidery hoops (4–6"/10–15 cm) in diameter) are perfect for small to medium embroidery projects and are easier to handle than larger hoops.

3 Loosen the screw on the outer embroidery hoop and separate it from the inner hoop. Lay your fabric on top of the inner hoop, open the outer hoop as wide as possible, and push it down over the inner hoop. Tighten the screw on the hoop.

4 Next you'll need to make sure your fabric is ready to work. Alternate pulling the fabric taut around the hoop and re-tightening the screw, as needed, until your fabric is completely wrinkle free within the hoop.

EMBROIDERY

5 *Backstitch*: Bring your needle up from the back of the fabric and pull through until the end knot is flush against the back of the fabric. Bring your needle back down into the fabric one stitch length away (about ⅛–¼ inch/3–6 mm, or the length of a grain of rice). Bring the needle back up one stitch length further down your pattern line and then take it back down through the last hole of the previous stitch. Continue working along your pattern. Take the needle to the back of the fabric, separate the strands of floss, and tie a knot to finish. Clip the threads close to the knot.

6 *Stem stitch*: Bring your needle up at the left-hand end of your stitching line and pull the floss all the way through until the knot is flush against the back of the fabric. Move to the right by two stitch lengths and insert your needle, bringing it immediately back up at the midway point between the two stitches. Repeat along the stitch line until you reach the end. Take the needle to the back of the fabric, separate the strands of floss, and tie a knot to finish. Clip the threads close to the knot.

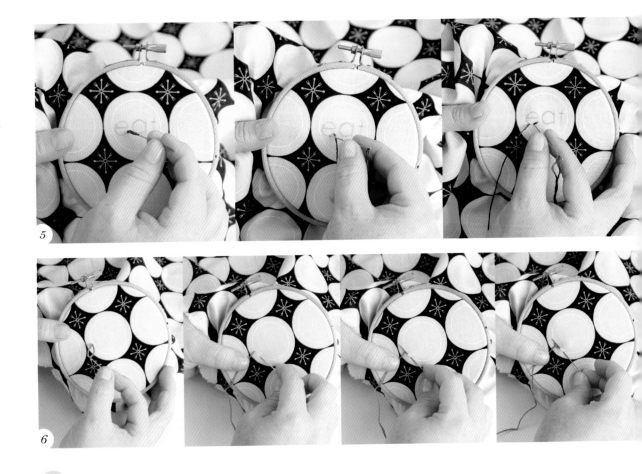

Hints and tips

Keep your length of embroidery floss no longer than about 16" (40 cm) (approximately the distance from your fingertips to your lower bicep). Longer threads can tangle easily while stitching.

You can separate out six individual strands of cotton embroidery floss to suit the look you hope to achieve (delicate vs. bold).

7 *Satin stitch*: Bring your needle up on the pattern line at the bottom center of the shape to be filled. Take your needle down, back directly across on the shape. Bring the needle back up and take it down just to the right of your initial stitch and continue to fill the right side of the shape. Once you fill one side, come back up to the left of your initial stitch and work out to the other side. Take the needle to the back of the fabric, separate the strands of floss, and tie a knot to finish. Clip the threads close to the knot.

8 When the stitching is complete, remove the fabric from the hoop and press it with a medium/high heat iron from the wrong side of the fabric to remove hoop the marks.

7

8

BASIC CROSS-STITCH

1   Cut a length of embroidery floss about 16″ (40 cm) long and thread about 2″ (5 cm) of it through the eye of the tapestry needle.

2   Fold your aida cloth in half, open and fold in half in the other direction, and open to locate the center point of the fabric.

3   Loosen the screw on the outer embroidery hoop and separate it from the inner hoop. Lay your fabric on top of the inner hoop and then open the outer hoop as wide as possible and push it down over the inner hoop. Tighten the screw.

4   Next you'll need to make sure your fabric is ready to work. Alternate pulling the fabric taut around the hoop and re-tightening the screw as needed until your fabric is completely wrinkle-free within the hoop.

TOOLS AND MATERIALS
- Small embroidery scissors
- Cotton embroidery floss
- Tapestry needle
- Aida cloth for cross-stitch
- Embroidery hoop

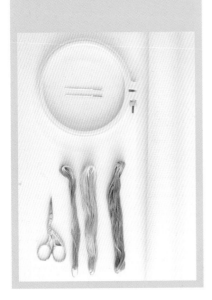

1

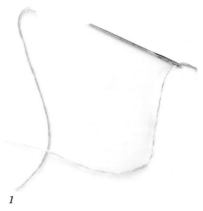

3

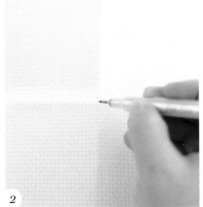

2

4

Hints and tips

Aida cloth comes in various count sizes of threads per square inch. This will affect the size of your finished piece, so plan accordingly.

Using a blunt-end tapestry needle keeps you from piercing the threads where you are not supposed to on the fabric.

Avoid pulling your stitches too tightly, causing gaps in your work.

When you are not working on your stitchery, loosen the embroidery hoop and remove your fabric to prevent permanent creasing.

5 Bring your needle up from behind the fabric, leaving about 1" (2.5 cm) of a tail of floss on the backside of the fabric. Secure the tail in the stitches as you work.

6 Work stitches according to pattern, always keeping the crosses going in the same direction.

7 Go back through your row of stitches and complete the other arm of the cross in the opposite direction.

8 To finish a section of stitches, take your needle to the backside of the fabric and thread it through the backside of stitches. Snip the excess floss with your embroidery scissors.

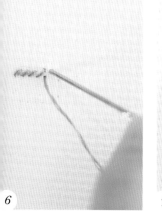

5

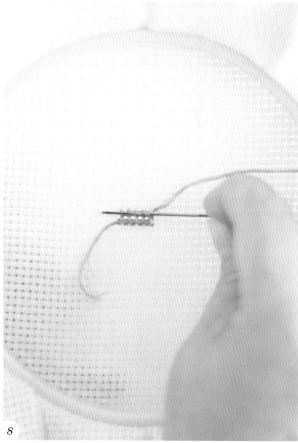

8

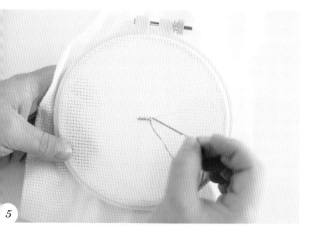

6

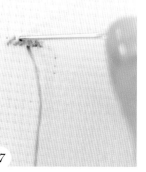

7

APPLIQUÉ

1   Pick an element of your print to use as your appliqué motif, and use the fabric scissors to cut out a piece of the fusible webbing that will accommodate that design.

2   Place the fusible webbing, adhesive side down, onto the wrong side of your fabric to be appliquéd.

3   Using a hot, completely dry iron, adhere the fusible webbing to the appliqué design. Refer to manufacturer instructions for the length of time needed to completely fuse the webbing.

4   Let the paper of the fusible webbing cool completely, and then cut your design element out using your paper scissors to avoid dulling your fabric shears.

TOOLS AND MATERIALS

- Fabric with which to appliqué
- Fabric scissors
- Paper-backed fusible webbing
- Iron
- Paper scissors
- Embroidery floss
- Embroidery scissors
- Pressing cloth (optional)

1

2

3

4

Hints and tips

Bold-printed fabrics lend themselves well to appliqué. Simply pick an element of the print you love, and cut it out to appliqué on a solid or complementing print fabric.

Fusible webbing comes in varying weights. Select light-, medium-, or heavyweight webbing that matches the functionality of the finished project.

Pressing cloths can be used to avoid getting any excess webbing adhesive on your ironing board cover or iron.

Hand or machine stitching can further secure your appliqué motif to your project, and can also be used as an additional decorative element.

5 Gently peel away the paper backing of the fusible webbing from your design. Your fabric now has a layer of adhesive on the back side.

6 Place the design, adhesive side down, on the base fabric for your project. Adhere the design using a gentle pressing motion with a hot, dry iron. Allow to cool.

7 Choose a complementing embroidery floss to embellish and further secure your design to the base fabric.

8 Once the appliqué design has adhered to the based fabric, you can further secure it or embellish it with the embroidery stitches from pages 134–135.

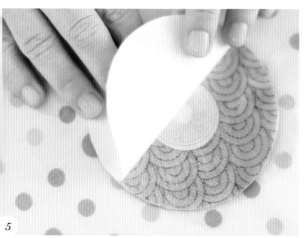

5

6

7

8

SPECIALIST
TECHNIQUES

Gallery

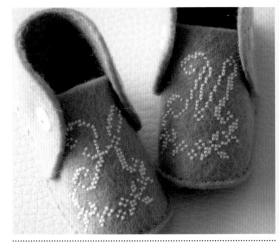

Mini baby shoes ornament handstitched from felt with cross-stitched initials. By Ayako mato Uemura

A steel wire armature frames this hand-embroidered, wool felt, stuffed skull decoration. Felt appliqué and vintage buttons add to the details of this mixed media sugar skull wall art. By Robin Romain

Perspective fiber art. Appliqué, patchwork, and handstitching. By Karen Turner

Freehand machine embroidery framed in a hoop. By Annabelle Ozanne

Floss embroidery on black-and-white fabric, which was embellished and stitched into a laptop sleeve. Embroidered and sewn by Lynn Harris. Nethercote fabric by Cloud 9 Fabrics. Laptop pattern by Keyka Lou

Freehand machine embroidery framed in a hoop.
By Annabelle Ozanne

Hand-embroidered soft sculpture houses. By Elena Klimora

Hand-embroidered brooches made using upcycled vintage linen. By Heleen Webb

Daisy chain ABC sampler. Uses a variety of crewel embroidery stitches. Stitched by Lynn Harris.
Kit designed by Alicia Paulson of Posie Gets Cozy

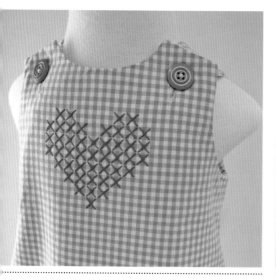

Infant's shirt dress with cross-stitched heart. By Rachel Winter

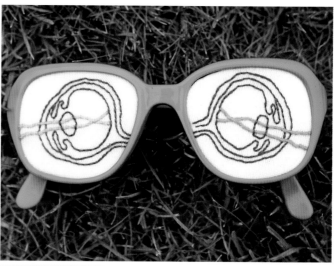

Diagram of the human eye, embroidered onto canvas and framed in a pair of recolored vintage spectacles. By Kirsty Neale

Hand-embroidered zip pouches made using upcycled vintage linen. By Heleen Webb

Multi-layered felted geode ball from wool roving. By Leah Adams

Wall-hanging with crochet and embroidered flowers. By Maria Rosa Lacerda Lage

RACHEL HOBSON

Interview

Rachel Hobson is a freelance craft writer and editor who is obsessed with hand embroidery and all things geektastic and funny. She has a passion for creating community through crafting. Rachel is also a huge space geek, and enjoys living five minutes from Houston's Johnson Space Center where she can get her fill of rockets any time she pleases.

averagejanecrafter.com

Can you describe your studio/work space?

I was extremely lucky to find a spectacular 1961 atomic ranch home when we moved to Houston. The woman who had lived there for more than forty years was an artist, and added on a massive studio and darkroom in the mid-1970s. The room is surrounded by massive floor-to-ceiling windows that look out on to the pine-tree-flanked swimming pool, and large dark beams punctuate the ceiling. It's no surprise that I never want to leave this space!

Are you formally trained as an artist/designer?

I stumbled in to stitchery after my mother gave me a sewing machine when I was pregnant with my second child. After I took my first embroidery class, it was like a floodgate of a lifetime of pent-up craftiness had been opened. I found a new obsession that hasn't died down since! I've taken many hand embroidery and surface design classes, and was a hand embroidery instructor in Austin, Texas, for almost three years.

Wool felt design elements are appliquéd on to patterned fabric with hand embroidery stitches to create a rich and colorful plush owl.

"My high texture hand embroidery of the moon is most special to me, because it was a piece I designed and stitched in a way I hadn't done anything before."

This high-texture hand embroidery of the moon won the 2D art first prize in the Etsy/NASA Space Craft contest, and a print of the piece flew into space onboard the last space shuttle ever launched. Photo by Jote Khalsa.

Embroidery is not limited to simple fabrics! If you can get your needle and thread through the material, you can embroider it. This lampshade was embellished with very simple stitches for a custom design.

Do you consider yourself a generalist or a specialist?

I guess I'd say I'm a specialist in needlework, but I love to explore all kinds of surface design. Handstitching just seems to really suit me, and I love learning and using all the different ways to embellish with stitchery.

Please describe your work and the materials you generally use.

I typically use cottons or linen fabrics on which I stitch with six-stranded cotton embroidery or pearl cotton floss. I occasionally use silk ribbon or crewel wool for stitching.

What other creative pursuits do you practice?

I love working with screen printing and fabric dyeing. I'm also a writer.

Is there a piece you're most proud of?

My high texture hand embroidery of the moon is most special to me, because it was a piece I designed and stitched in a way I hadn't done anything before. It pushed me outside my comfort zone and helped me take my work to a whole new level. The piece went on to win a contest and a print of the embroidery flew into space on the last space shuttle ever launched.

Where do you find inspiration?

Most of my inspiration comes from my deep passion for space exploration. I love studying astronomy and planetary science and keeping up with what's going on in spaceflight. Sharing this knowledge through my art is one of my greatest joys. I also love reading any kind of stitchery book, and have amassed quite a collection of vintage hand embroidery books.

It was like a floodgate of a lifetime of pent-up craftiness had been opened. I found a new obsession that hasn't died down since! "

Patterned fabrics are a great place for punchneedle embroidery. You can use the printed designs as the framework for your stitches.

Store-bought tea towels can be easily updated for the holidays with simple words printed from a computer, transferred on, and then stitched.

What do you do if you're feeling uninspired or stuck?

I love to pick up one of my embroidery books and thumb through the pages, or go onto the Internet and look at images of embroidery. Something about just seeing pictures of stitches makes me want to grab my needle and get to work. Sometimes I'll put a scrap piece of cloth in my hoop and use it as a doodle cloth to just practice stitches or just stitch without having to have a specific project in mind.

Do you sell any of your work? How do you market yourself?

I do not currently sell my work, but I share my work through my blog and various social media outlets.

Despite its delicate appearance, hand embroidery is actually quite sturdy and a practical way to embellish everyday items, like dish towels.

From a journalist's perspective, do you have advice for artists who are starting out regarding how to market and sell their work?

Find your passion and run with it. Be true to yourself and don't get caught up in what other people are saying or doing. Have fun, and avoid the pressures of perfection at all costs. Just enjoy!

What do you see next for you and your career?

I have an art collection in the works, and I'd love to write a book to go along with it. I'm also planning on getting back to teaching embroidery (something that brings me great joy) very soon!

Are there any new techniques you'd like to try?

I've dabbled in fabric dyeing before, but not to the level I'd really like to explore. I'm fascinated by being able to create custom textiles onto which I could stitch.

Circles of hand-dyed fabrics (representing the planets in the solar system) were appliquéd onto this skirt to represent the fabric of the cosmos.

This sweet image was part of a vintage embroidery kit that was found, unstitched, at a thrift store. The sequins add a special sparkle.

"Find your passion and run with it. Be true to yourself and don't get caught up in what other people are saying or doing."

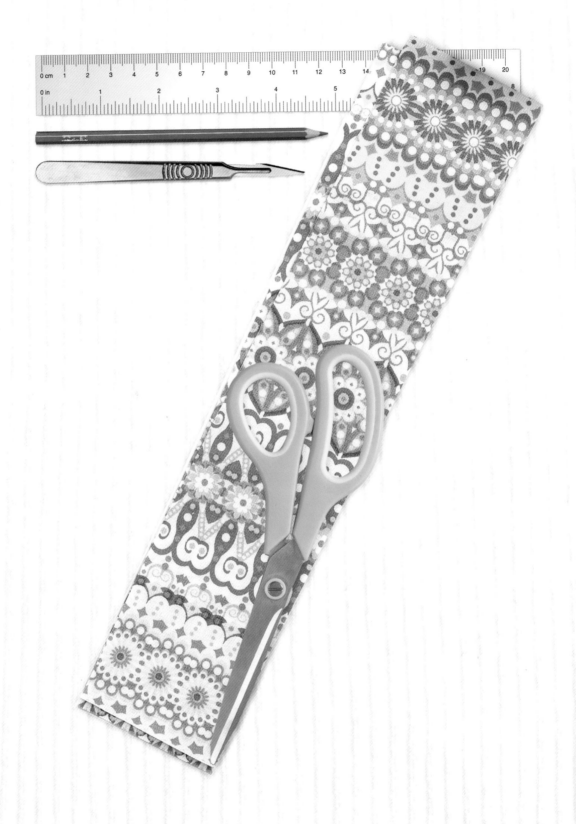

7 GOING PRO

by Laurie Wisbrun

After mastering the embellishment techniques in this book, you may want to take the next step by turning professional and selling your work. With the rise of digital printing services, online marketplaces, and social media networks, there has never been a better time to take the plunge with going pro.

I was fortunate enough to be able to include the work of three amazing artists who have taken the art of embellishing fabric to the next level. In this chapter you'll gain some insight into what inspires them, how they work, and how they market their work.

TIPS FOR GOING PRO

If you're considering taking your embellishing and work with textiles to the marketplace and selling it, there are a wide variety of elements to consider related to your designs, production, and marketing.

Working with a digital printing service

Much of the commercially printed fabric you see in the store has been screen-printed in large quantities in a mill. If you're anxious to see what your patterns will look like on fabric, digitally printing it in small quantities may be a great option for you.

The last several years has seen a great deal of growth in the print-on-demand sector for digitally printed textiles. These services allow individual designers, crafters, and DIYers to print their own fabric in very small quantities at reasonable cost.

Patterns can be printed on a wide variety of basecloths that range from lightweight cottons to silks, rayons, and heavyweight canvas. The way the process works is that you upload your digital file to the company's website and generally within a few weeks your fabric will be printed and shipped directly to you. Each service will have its own file specifications and instructions, so it's wise to spend some time reading the getting started documentation on the company's website to learn how to prepare your digital files.

Licensing your designs

If producing your own fabric isn't an avenue you're interested in exploring but you have dreams of seeing your designs on fabric or other goods, you might consider licensing your patterns. Most fabric manufacturers—especially in the quilting and craft sector—have in-house designers, but will also work with outside designers for their art. There are also many companies who manufacture goods from textiles (think bedding, sleepwear, clothing, bags, etc.) who commission designs from independent artists.

When an artist licenses their artwork, it means the manufacturer is paying the artist for the right to use the artist's designs on the goods they manufacture. Contracts are generally structured to pay the artist either a flat fee or to pay royalties against sales.

Licensing research

If you're interested in exploring licensing, I highly recommend the following resources:

- *Licensing Art & Design: A Professional's Guide to Licensing and Royalty Agreements.* Caryn R. Leland. Allworth Press, 1995.

- Join a discussion group online where you can learn from other artists and experts in the field, for example the Art of Licensing group on LinkedIn (linkedin.com)

- Do an internet search for blogs which focus on licensing art

- Attend an art licensing event, such as Surtex (surtex.com)

Developing a collection

If you choose to sell your work, you'll need to decide if you are creating items which are stand-alone individual pieces or if you'll be marketing them as part of a collection. A collection should make a strong statement about your unique style and your brand and should tell a cohesive story. Once you think your collection is ready for production, spend some time looking at it with a critical eye and edit, edit, edit.

At this stage, you'll also want to do your homework on where you'll source your materials, work out your production costs, determine your pricing, and decide how you'll be marketing your goods. A brilliant resource for understanding how to take your designs and turn them into a marketable business is a book called *Craft, Inc.: The Ultimate Guide to Turning Your Creative Hobby into a Successful Business* by Meg Mateo Ilasco.

Marketing and selling your designs

Online marketplaces—Online marketplaces have really leveled the playing field for independent artists. They're a great, low cost way to set up an online store that already has a base of customers looking for handmade goods. You will still need to build awareness about your store, but the effort will be worth it as these sites have millions of members who shop on a regular basis.

Blogs—If you have the time and inclination, setting up your own blog is a great way to promote your fledgling business. However, you can also consider contributing to other people's blogs. The craft community is overflowing with bloggers from all over the world sharing information and inspiration with each other. When you have news to share, send a few images and a quick summary of your work to a handful of bloggers where you think your work might fit. Having your work featured on a popular blog can expose your work to a new audience who might not have been familiar with you.

Social networking sites—It seems that social media is growing exponentially each day and there are a variety of tools you can use to show your work with more and more people. These tools are a great way to share a bit more about who you are (the person behind the business), how you spend your days, your working process, and exciting happenings with your business. Make sure you spend some time reading the terms and conditions of each site so that you're aware of how your images can be used once they've been uploaded.

DIGITAL PRINTING SERVICES
Several companies to consider are:
- Spoonflower
  spoonflower.com
- Fabric on Demand
  fabricondemand.com
- Stoff'n
  stoffn.de

POPULAR ONLINE MARKETPLACES
- Dawanda
  dawanda.com
- Envelop
  envelop.com
- Etsy
  etsy.com
- Spoonflower
  spoonflower.com
- Zazzle
  zazzle.com

POPULAR SOCIAL NETWORKS
- Facebook
  facebook.com
- Flickr
  flickr.com
- LinkedIn
  linkedin.com
- Pinterest
  pinterest.com
- Twitter
  twitter.com

TARA BADCOCK

Interview

Tara Badcock is an Australian textile artist, currently based in Tasmania after several years in Paris working within her design identity, Tara Badcock PARIS+TASMANIA. Individual pieces range from artworks, homewares, fashion, and accessories, to her ongoing Teacosy* Revolution project. Tara has built a strong reputation for her unique art textiles and is fast becoming recognized internationally for her combination of textile manipulation, and stitching and hand embroidery techniques. Her work is also featured in a number of collections, including the Tasmanian Museum and Art Gallery in Hobart, and UNESCO's Collection Permanent in Paris.

paristasmania.com
flickr.com/photos/tarabadcock/
teacosyrevolutiontara.blogspot.com

Where are you located?

I live with my partner Rainier and our son, Felix, in Deloraine, in Northern Tasmania, Australia. My studio is on the top floor of the converted nineteenth-century brick flour mill we're living in. I have great views over all our neighbors' gardens, the surrounding hills, and mountain range nearby.

How would you describe your work and technique?

I'm really passionate about working with hand embroidery as it creates such a varied and textured surface and imagery can become so three-dimensional. Hand embroidery is seen as something for grandmas, outdated and unnecessary in our modern lives full of computer-generated embroidery and fabric embellishments.

I've started using more freehand machine embroidery as I'm able to create imagery more quickly by machine than by hand embroidering it, and also because it satisfies my need to draw! I really love the quality both hand and freehand machine embroidery gives to the surface of fabrics and layers of fabrics. I'm not a purist nor perfectionist when it comes to making my textile pieces—I don't use a hoop or frame to embroider with, because I like the sculptural quality I can achieve by embroidering freehand.

Majestic India cushion. Freehand machine embroidery on silk with printed Pippijoe hemp backing and vintage buttons.

Female Scarlet Robin panel. Freehand machine and hand embroidery on silk, wool, and Japanese cotton.

Dress Circle cushion. Hand embroidery on silk with Tasmanian wool padding, and hemp jacquard backing.

Are you formally trained as an artist?

I trained at art school doing an honors degree in printmaking, specializing in stone lithography. I'd been printing lithographs onto silk and making sculptural garments out of them, but once I left uni, I didn't have the money to start my own lithography studio, and wasn't sure I wanted to be so settled at that stage. So although I come from a printmaking and drawing background, with a healthy dose of graphic design (hence my love of typography and text!), for me, embroidery offers really exciting ways of embedding imagery into and onto fabrics.

Where do you find inspiration?

Everywhere! I think everything I own falls into William Morris's maxim: "Have nothing in your house that you do not know to be useful, or believe to be beautiful." I've spent my life looking for beautiful, useful things to fill my home with and provide constant inspiration.

I also find an enormous amount of inspiration on my daily walks with my son, chatting to people, looking in op shops (thrift stores), taking walks in the bush looking for animal bones and interesting seed pods . . . it's hard to think of a moment when I'm not seeking inspiration. An artist's life is not a job, nor a career; it's more of a calling and is self-nourishing and sustaining.

Hand-embroidered silk bodice, silk ruffle skirt, and hand-embroidered silk satin breastplate, linen and silk pinafore dress, hand-embroidered linen chemise with buttoned shoulder straps.
Photo © Brad Hick/Six6

"I'm not a purist nor perfectionist when it comes to making my textile pieces—I don't use a hoop or frame to embroider with, because I like the sculptural quality I can achieve by embroidering freehand."

Australian Raven. Freehand machine embroidery on silk, Tasmanian wool and cotton, with glass bead eye.

"I don't always get the insights into a piece if I'm not able to work on it from start to finish. Each piece has to be allowed to go along its own path to its final stage, to have its own adventure and evolve its own personality."

What do you do if you're feeling uninspired or stuck?

I go for a walk and look at what's happening in the natural world. I look through my library to see what sticks out to catch my attention. Since childhood, I've collected a vast array of images/texts/ideas/memories/objects, which I've always felt I've been storing away for future reference.

The most valuable piece of advice my lithography lecturer gave me was to make a collage and just play whenever I felt stuck and uninspired. I do regularly, and now make more fabric collages, which is why my work features a lot of overlaid and patched-looking fabrics. I find collage always gets things flowing in exciting new directions.

Shoulder bag and embroidered silk rosette for Baz Luhrmann's film set of The Great Gatsby.

When you're creating a piece, how closely do you follow a vision/plan? Or does the piece evolve as you work?

I often start with either a sketchy design or a few words to direct me, or a detailed sketch if a piece is commissioned by a customer. In either case, a piece always evolves as I work on it, because the actual process of making is intrinsic to my artistic vision. This is why, even though I'd love lots of help making my work, I don't always get the insights into a piece if I'm not able to work on it from start to finish. Each piece has to be allowed to go along its own path to its final stage, to have its own adventure and evolve its own personality.

Bohemian Teaparty. Grace Cossington-Smith purse 2009. Hand and freehand machine embroidered silk, wool, and linen with leather backing.

Can you tell me about your Teacosy* Revolution project?

The Teacosy* Revolution is meant to rescue the humble tea cosy from the musty drawers of domestic life to give it a new spin: the tea cosy as sculptural form and revolutionary catalyst of debate. I started making tea cosies when I lived in Paris, which helped alleviate my homesickness and linked me to cultural practices from my home country... and so I decided to mount a Revolution. The basic idea is to give tea cosies a cultural platform within contemporary society; to acknowledge their function as a social focal point from an Australian historical viewpoint, and to carry that through to contemporary popular culture and our common desire for comfort and familiarity. It's both an experiment in the uses of thread and a forum for the merging threads of new conversation in contemporary crafts discourse. It's a movement dedicated to sharing, teaching, learning, experimenting, challenging, and updating traditional techniques and social forms of interaction and communication. Viva la Revolution with a nice hot cup of oh-so-glorious tea!

Flame Robin Freehand machine embroidery on silk, Tasmanian wool and cotton.

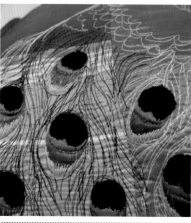

Detail of Majestic India cushion.

Embroidery detail.

There's No Place Like Home cosy. Patchwork blocks with a mixture of hand and freehand machine embroidery, referencing Tara's grandmother's handwriting.

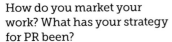
Gray-breasted bird panel. Freehand machine and hand embroidery on silk, wool, and cotton.

Common Myna. Freehand machine embroidery on silk, Tasmanian wool and cotton, with hand-embroidered highlights.

How do you market your work? What has your strategy for PR been?

When I moved back to Tasmania, I enrolled in a small business course to help me structure my business approach and get some insight into what I needed to do with the financial side of things. At the same time I was meeting retailers and gallery owners to try and get my work into these environments.

One of the best shops that stocks my work, Planet Commonwealth in Sydney (a groovy and divine arty interiors store), bought some cushions as a starter and one of them turned up in a magazine a few months later! That spurred me on to contact magazines directly and keep sending them images of current collections, to plant seeds and get them acquainted with my work. I've also been introduced to journalists, stylists, and photographers. The great thing is that, when you're on this path, something always happens because you're actively attracting this kind of interest. I also engaged a public relations professional to help get my name out there and sell more pieces and whole collections.

Some essential advice for marketing: make sure you have really good, professional-looking images of your work, in both high- and low-resolution format, to easily supply to magazine stylists, editors, journalists, retailers, etc., so that your work looks the best it can as a two-dimensional image.

If you're pitching your work at a particular magazine, find out which future issues will include themes that fit with your work, then get in touch with the relevant features editor. This information is often included in an online editorial calendar. Since they are often working months in advance, make sure you approach them at least three months in advance of the issue. Don't be offended if your work doesn't end up appearing—magazines are big businesses and don't have time to be sentimental!

Boobook Owl brooch. Freehand machine- and hand-embroidered silk, wool, leather, and safety pin.

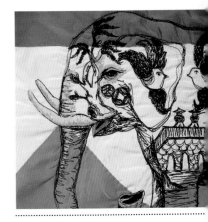
East India Elephant Cushion. Hand and freehand machine embroidery on silk with printed cotton backing and vintage buttons.

Do you have any advice on pricing?

I got some good advice from an artist who was endeavoring to make a living from her work as a potter. She said to decide what sort of income you'd like to make a week (inclusive of costs), break that down into a nine-to-five working day and week, and then you can work out your hourly rate.

This helped me to price my work in the beginning. I sat down one day to dedicate myself wholly to making one hand-embroidered cushion from start to finish, to time it and cost the materials and calculate my working hours. From there I could set myself a general price range for each type of item I make. I also believe I need to be as flexible with pricing as possible and not get too greedy, even if it means changing the way I create each piece. The positive side of this is that it keeps my work fresh and invigorated with some sort of enduring cultural relevance, which in my work is important as I'm aiming to create works that are heirlooms and future collector's pieces.

Another simple approach is to calculate your costs—materials, overheads, packaging, and freight—for each item, then triple it to get your wholesale price. Once I figure out a good bread-and-butter line that extracts minimal costs for the highest return for me, that'll be my couture line that funds the rest of the business!

"I'm aiming to create works that are heirlooms and future collector's pieces."

What do you see next for you and your career?

In addition to building my online store, I would love to find people I can employ to help me so I'm able to spend time with my son and on the artwork side of my practice. I'm planning to work toward regular, small collections of clothing and I also want to apply my textiles to furniture and fittings.

I have a long-held desire to publish a book of the Teacosy* Revolution Manifesto. Its something I've been working on slowly for the past few years and I'd really like to get it finished and printed before I'm old and gray!

Spice Island purse. Freehand machine embroidery and hand embroidery on silk, with leather body and Japanese silk lining, silk rosette, hemp string, and metal clasp.

Our Lady of Arcadia; Empress. Torso detail. Freehand machine embroidery, hand embroidery, silk, wool, cotton, antique pressed glass and shell and steel buttons, galah feather.

LOUISE RICHARDSON

Interview

Louise Richardson's work has evolved through a process of discovery and investigation. Collecting ideas and materials enables her to build up a library of resources to draw upon for each new piece. Her work is centered around the ideas of memory and identity, bringing universal messages to the viewer, through the portrayal of objects in her own memory. The diversity of materials within her work—both found and processed—gives her the opportunity and freedom to invent metaphors that run parallel with the subject matter. She is based in England and works in a studio she describes as "messy and eclectic," which she shares with her children's two guinea pigs.

flickr.com/photos/louiserichardsonart

Are you formally trained as an artist?

After school, I spent two years on a foundational course of generalized art learning. After completing that, I went onto a three-year degree course in fine art, specializing in painting. I spent the next several years working in a studio and teaching art courses, then went back to college to complete an MA in fine art. Since then I've worked independently for exhibitions and taught in various schools and colleges.

What materials do you usually work with?

Lots and lots! I tend to be very eclectic and my studio is full of boxes with materials and objects that I feel will be useful, although I think the common link is a certain aesthetic or feel. After a time you learn to identify the potential of certain materials, whether it's a box of dandelion clocks or a packet of nails. Also, the reinterpretation of materials is very important for my work.

Charm. Mixed media and shed snake skin.

Spellbound. Mixed media and butterflies.

Nettle. Mixed media and butterflies.

Do you consider yourself a generalist or a specialist?

I would say I'm a generalist because my ideas tend to lead and the materials follow. Although within the realms of my practice, there is specialty in the techniques I apply to my work.

Where do you find inspiration?

Anywhere. Although my work deals with identity and memory, an idea for a piece can come from an object, an item of clothing, a photograph, or a story. Something will create a spark that kindles a story or an opportunity for a new piece of work.

What do you do if you're feeling uninspired or stuck?

Rummage is a good word to describe what I do. Whether it's rummaging through the boxes in my studio, through my head for ideas and memories, or through books or junk shops . . . something usually happens! Often I will just start making and see where it leads.

When you're creating a piece, how closely do you follow a vision/plan? Or does the piece evolve as you work?

I tend to have an idea or feeling at the start of a piece, although often you have to follow the work as it evolves—it creates its own history, which adds another dimension to the work.

How do you market and sell your work?

I primarily sell through galleries and exhibitions, often one tends to lead to another. The use of Flickr.com has resulted in numerous contacts and a real variety of opportunities, so I consider it part of my marketing efforts.

"You have to follow the work as it evolves—it creates its own history, which adds another dimension."

Unsettle. Mixed media and paper butterflies.

Settle. Mixed media and paper butterflies.

LUCIE SUMMERS

Interview

Lucie Summers is a designer who loves color and pattern. A mixed media artist, she designs and sells hand screen-printed fabric as well as prints and household goods through her Etsy store. In partnership with Moda, she launched her first commercially available fabric line, Summersville. She finds inspiration in flowers and leaves, vintage papers, block printing, and more.

summersville.etsy.com

Where are you located?

I live on a farm in a small village just outside a town called Newmarket in Suffolk in the United Kingdom. And when I say small, I mean no shops—just a pub. But we're close to lots of lovely cities, like Cambridge and Norwich, and central London is just an hour's train ride away.

Provide a brief description of your work and your technique.

Much of my work begins life as a little sketch with black pens. If I like what I'm doing, I might extend the drawing to a larger piece of paper. If I can see it working as a screen print, I'll scan the drawing and work on the repeat in Photoshop. I then send the design away to be put on to a screen. When the screen arrives, I experiment with different ink colors and generally have a play. It's the best moment!

Are you formally trained as an artist?

I went to art school in Norwich, where I specialized in printmaking. After I graduated, I opened a patchwork and quilting shop with my mum called The Colour Room. In those days, stores like ours weren't the norm—we ran workshops and had a huge array of fabric. Funnily enough, it was a bad time for me creatively. Being in the shop all day, helping out other people, meant I was exhausted and didn't feel like doing anything when I got home. Luckily, my enthusiasm for being creative came back after I had children!

"I'm a magpie for interesting old bowls, ceramics, pots, and knick-knacks and a lot of inspiration and pleasure comes from arranging them around the house."

"Much of my work begins life as a little sketch with black pens. If I like what I'm doing I might extend the drawing to a larger piece of paper. If I can see it working as a screen print, I'll scan the drawing and work on the repeat in Photoshop."

Double-sided gift wrap in Totem print.

Where do you find inspiration?

I am very fortunate to live in a lovely part of the world with big open skies and tons of countryside. And living on a farm, the outdoors is a big part of the life—leaves, flowers, and texture feature heavily in my designs. Another big inspiration are the things I pick up in thrift stores. I'm a magpie for interesting old bowls, ceramics, pots, and knick-nacks and a lot of inspiration and pleasure comes from arranging them around the house.

What do you do if you're feeling uninspired or stuck?

I'm addicted to Pinterest and find it endlessly inspiring. I like Flickr.com for looking at people's quilts, and reading blogs. I'm an avid collector of U.S. shelter magazines and keep most of them, so I'll flick through them until something sparks my interest. When all else fails, I walk across the fields to clear my head. It works every time.

Vinyl sticky tape featuring Bloomsbury print.

Bone china mug featuring Bloomsbury print.

Summersville fabric for Moda.

How do you market your work?

I've always used Etsy as my main selling space. I've tried other avenues, but none have been quite as successful for me. I'll be truthful: I'm a lazy marketer. I'm not a fan of Facebook, but I do like Twitter. When I've got something new to share, it's the first place I'll go to shout about it. Then, fingers crossed, it'll get re-tweeted by other people and you'll reach another audience. Word of mouth is a powerful thing. Posting regularly on Flickr helps too, and I have a blog. I try not to go on and on about my work constantly though, otherwise it's just too boring. I know that using these sites has not only driven people to buy my work, but they've also led to other types of work. A few years ago I created a series of collages for New York stationery company Gallison, and I designed some fabric for Clothkits, a clothing company.

Lucie's studio gets tons of light from the sash windows and has plenty of built-in storage.

Describe your first fabric collection with Moda.

The first collection, Summersville, is a group of prints I was already selling through Etsy. I sent Moda fourteen or so designs and they chose eight they liked best. The scales were changed a little, which looks great. I'm so used to using small pieces of my printed fabric that working with yardage is really exciting!

Lucie keeps a large board for pinning inspirational items from magazines, as well as printed and sewn samples.

> "*I think it's very important to send emails to blogs you actually read. Sounds simple, but imagine how irritating it is for blog authors to have inboxes jammed full of people getting their names wrong!*"

Summersville fabric for Moda.

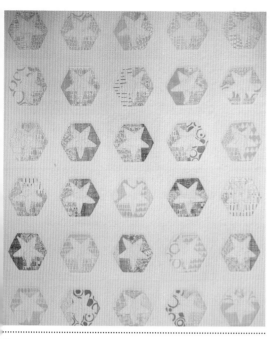

Hexagons and Stars quilt made for The Festival of Quilts 2011. Pieced by Lucie and longarm quilted by Jenny Spencer.

Chevron quilt made from strike-offs of Summersville line. Designed and pieced by Lucie Summers. Quilted by Jenny Spencer.

You work a lot with your mother, who does your quilting. How did that partnership come to be?

When we had The Colour Room, we also were the first shop in the area to import a longarm quilting machine and to offer quilting services. My mum has more than ten years' experience and her work is amazing. I'm incredibly lucky to have her work on my quilts, because I don't enjoy quilting on a regular machine. Working together was a no-brainer really! She has now pretty much retired from quilting regularly, but she does it for friends and for me. I also respect her advice over piecing the quilt too—after all, she's been doing it for a lot longer than I have! It's very useful to have somebody to bounce ideas off. It's quite isolating working on your own, so I appreciate the discussions.

You've received some wonderful press coverage. What was your strategy for your public relations?

I've been lucky enough to have been featured on several well-known and established design blogs, such as *Design*Sponge, decor8, print & pattern*, and *True Up*, to name a few. Sometimes I'm lucky enough to have things written about me and it's a lovely surprise; other times I send a brief and friendly email to blog authors with links to my new work.

What advice do you have for artists who are starting out regarding how to market and promote their work?

Sending emails to blog authors is a great way for people to find out about you—it's important that your email is straight to the point, but at the same time sounds approachable. Don't send lots of copy-and-pasted emails at the same time to different blogs. I find the most relevant sites for my work, and if I don't have a response after three or four days, I send one to another.

I think it's very important to send emails to blogs you actually read. Sounds simple, but imagine how irritating it is for blog authors to have inboxes jammed full of people getting their names wrong! Most of the big blogs have submission guidelines, so take the time to read through them carefully.

Utilizing all the social networking sites is another must. Twitter definitely gets me sales, but again, you need to tweet about other things too—not just your work. People will get bored and unfollow you. I actually think it's best if you're relaxed about your work. Nothing's more of a turnoff than desperation.

DYEING CHARTS

Making Natural Dyes

Fabric	Mordant Alum	Mordant Cream of tartar	Dye Light Shade	Dye Medium Shade	Dye Dark Shade
¼ yd (0.22 m)	½ tsp (2.5 ml)	¼ tsp (1.25ml)	½ tbsp (7.5 ml)	1¼ tbsp (18.7 ml)	2 tbsp (30 ml)
½ yd (0.45 m)	1 tsp (5 ml)	½ tsp (2.5 ml)	1 tbsp (15 ml)	2½ tbsp (37.5 ml)	4 tbsp (60 ml)
1 yd (0.9 m)	2 tsp (10 ml)	1 tsp (5 ml)	2 tbsp (30 ml)	5 tbsp (75 ml)	8 tbsp (120 ml)

Natural Dye Colors

Dyestuff	Color
alkanet	purple
annatto	yellow
brazilwood	pink–rose
cochineal	red–violet
cutch	yellow–tan–brown
henna	brown
kamala	yellow
logwood	purple–brown
madder	pink–red
osage orange sawdust	yellow–orange
sandalwood	orange

Mixing Chemical Dyebaths and Solutions

Fabric	¼ yd (0.22 m)	½ yd (0.45 m)	1 yd (0.9 m)
Start water	1 cup (240 ml)	2 cups (480 ml)	4 cups (960 ml)
Salt	2½ tbsp (37.5 ml)	5 tbsp (75 ml)	10 tbsp (150 ml)
Urea	1 tsp (5 ml)	2 tsp (10 ml)	4 tsp (20 ml)
Dye: pale shade	⅟₁₆ tsp (0.3 ml)	⅛ tsp (0.6 ml)	¼ tsp (1.25 ml)
Dye: light shade	⅛ tsp (0.6 ml)	¼ tsp (1.25 ml)	½ tsp (2.5 ml)
Dye: medium shade	¼ tsp (1.25 ml)	½ tsp (2.5 ml)	1 tsp (5 ml)
Dye: deep shade	½ tsp (2.5 ml)	1 tsp (5 ml)	2 tsp (10 ml)
Dye: dark shade	1 tsp (5 ml)	2 tsp (10 ml)	4 tsp (20 ml)
Dye activator	1½ tsp (7.5 ml)	1 tbsp (15 ml)	2 tbsp (30 ml)

Tie-Dyeing

Intensity	Pale	Light
Dye	⅛ tsp (0.6 ml)	¼–½ tsp (1.25–2.5 ml)

Intensity	Medium	Dark
Dye	1–2 tsp (5–10 ml)	2–3 tsp (10–15 ml)

Bleaching: Dip/Vat

Intensity	Pale	Light
Dye	¼ tsp (1.25 ml)	½–1 tsp (2.5–5 ml)

Intensity	Medium	Dark
Dye	2–3 tsp (10–15 ml)	4–6 tsp (20–30 ml)

SUPPLIERS, MAGAZINES, BLOGS, AND BOOKS

General Supplies and Materials

Atlantis Art Materials & Art Supplies
atlantisart.co.uk

Brighton Sewing Centre
brightonsewingcentre.com

Dick Blick Art Materials
dickblick.com

Eckersley's Art & Craft
eckersleys.com.au

Hobby Lobby
hobbylobby.com

Hobby Craft
hobbycraft.co.uk

Jerry's Artarama
jerrysartarama.com

Jo-Ann Fabrics and Crafts
joann.com

Michael's Arts & Crafts Stores
michaels.com

Printing, Dyeing, and Fiber Supplies

Dharma Trading
dharmatrading.com

Dyeshop UK
dyeshop.co.uk

Earth Guild
earthguild.com

Prairie Point Junction
prairiepointjunction.com

Pro Chemical and Dye
prochemicalanddye.com

Silk Screening Supplies
silkscreeningsupplies.com

Spoonflower
spoonflower.com

Embellishment, Trim, and Patterns

Accessories of Old
accessoriesofold.com

Avenue 55
avenue55.etsy.com

Liberty of London
liberty.co.uk

Retro Na Na
retronana.etsy.com

Sublime Stitching
sublimestitching.com

V. V. Rouleaux
vvrouleaux.com

Magazines

Mollie Makes
molliemakes.com

Threads
threadsmagazine.com

Blogs

Craft Gossip
craftgossip.com

Craft Zine
craftzine.com

True Up
trueup.net

Books

The Complete Guide to Natural Dyeing.
Eva Lambert. Search Press, 2010.

Craft Inc.: The Ultimate Guide to Turning Your Creative Hobby into a Successful Business.
Meg Mateo Ilasco. Chronicle Books, 2011 (revised edition).

Creative Dyeing for Fabric Arts.
Suzanne McNeill. Design Originals, 2011.

The Embroidery Stitch Bible.
Betty Barnden. Krause Publications, 2003.

Fabricate: 17 Innovative Sewing Projects That Make Fabric the Star.
Susan Wasinger. Interweave Press, 2009.

Fabric Embellishing: The Basics & Beyond.
Liz Kettle, Heather Thomas, Ruth Chandler, Lauren Vlcek. Landauer Corporation, 2009.

The Handmade Marketplace: How to Sell Your Crafts Locally, Globally, and Online.
Kari Chapin. Storey Publishing, 2010.

Licensing Art & Design: A Professional's Guide to Licensing and Royalty Agreements.
Caryn R. Leland. Allworth Press, 1995.

Mastering the Art of Fabric Printing and Design.
Laurie Wisbrun. Chronicle Books, 2012.

Printing by Hand: A Modern Guide to Printing with Handmade Stamps, Stencils, and Silk Screens.
Lena Corwin. Stewart, Tabori & Chang, 2008.

Sew Wild: Creating with Stitch and Mixed Media.
Alisa Burke. Interweave Press, 2011.

GLOSSARY

Appliqué
A technique where one piece of fabric is layered onto another to create a design.

Auxillary chemicals
In fabric dyeing, chemicals used in conjunctions with dyes to fix the dye.

Batching
In dyeing, a process used after the dye has been applied to the fabric. The fabric sits in a warm and humid environment, which allows the chemical reaction between the dye, fiber, and auxilliary chemicals to fully exhaust themselves and set the dye.

Batik
A form of wax-resist dyeing.

Beading needle
A very fine needle designed to fit within the small holes of a bead.

Bleach pen
A laundry pen filled with bleach that allows for controlled application on fabrics.

Blended fabric
A fabric made from more than one type of fiber.

Block printing
A process for applying color using a carved block.

Brick repeat
A print layout where the elements are moved halfway down to the next image.

Cellulose fiber
Plant-based fibers, such as cotton and linen.

Cross-stitch
A type of embroidery where x-shaped stitches are combined to create images.

Cyanotype printing
A photographic printing process that utilizes the sun to create cyan-blue prints.

Dip dyeing
A process for submerging selected areas of fabric in a dye bath to achieve a new color.

Dip/vat bleaching
A process for submerging fabric in a bleach bath to remove or alter color.

Discharge paste
An agent used in dyeing to remove color from fabric.

Dye activator
Used to fix dye to fabric, making the color permanent.

Dyebox
Powdered dyes are mixed inside the box reducing the amount of dye that can become airborne.

Embroidery
A process of embellishing an item using embroidery floss, thread, or yarn.

Embroidery floss
Fibers (often six strands of cotton thread spun together) specifically for use in embroidery or other needlework.

Embroidery hoop
A tool for keeping fabric taut to enable working of embroidery or other handwork.

Fabric grain
All knit and woven fabric is made up of threads that run vertically and horizontally, creating the grain of the fabric. A lengthwise grain runs parallel to the fabric selvedges and has no stretch. A crosswise grain runs perpendicular to the fabric selvedges and has slight stretch.

Fusible webbing
A no-sew fiber that will melt when heated, bonding two pieces of fabric together.

Half-drop repeat
A print layout where the elements are moved halfway vertically to the next image.

Heat-transfer printing
A method for applying an image to fabric using heat.

Interfacing
Used in sewing to give an item more structure or to make an item more rigid.

Iron-on transfers
A method for applying a printed image to fabric through the application of heat.

Mordant
Substance used with natural dyes to set the color onto the fabric.

Motif
An element or shape that makes up a design or pattern.

Natural dyes
Dyes made from natural sources, such as plants or insects.

Natural fabric
A fabric made without any synthetic fibers.

Neutralizer
Used in dyeing to stop the process of removing color.

Over dyeing
The process of adding color on top of existing color.

Prepared for dyeing (PFD) fabric
Fabric that is unbleached and has an off-white color, which will take dyes better than non-PFD fabrics.

Protein fiber
Fibers made from animal sources, such as wool and silk.

Punchneedle
An embroidery technique that uses a special punchneedle tool to create loops on the front side of the fabric.

Resists
A method in dyeing to prevent the dye from reaching portions of the fabric.

Scale
Refers to the size of elements in a design.

Screen printing
A printing method where the pattern is applied by forcing ink through a screen that contains an ink blocking stencil.

Seed beads
Very tiny beads, which are generally round and made of glass.

Shibori
A type of fabric resist that creates a pattern through folding, crimping, compressing, or twisting to create areas where the dye cannot reach the fabric.

Sun-dyeing
A dyeing process that uses solar-activated dyes to create color and pattern.

Synthetic fabric
Fabric made from man-made fibers, such as nylon and acrylic.

Textile detergent
Used as a pre- and post-wash in dyeing.

Thread conditioner
A product that reduces tangling and friction when applied to thread or embroidery floss.

Tie-dyeing
A type of shibori dyeing.

Tile repeat
A print layout where the elements are aligned along vertical and horizontal lines.

Underlay
A piece of fabric or protectant paper placed under the item being printed. Used to protect your printing table or surface.

Urea water
Used to make the dye solution in techniques such as tie dye and dip dyeing, where the dye is applied directly to specific areas of the fabric. It serves as a humectant to keep the fabric damp enough for the dye reaction to occur.

INDEX

CONTRIBUTORS

Alicia Paulson, Posie Gets Cozy
aliciapaulson.com

Alison Tauber
alisontauber.com

Amy King
shinyorangedreams.blogspot.com

Andrea Whalen
spoonflower.com/profiles/domesticate

Andrea M. Wolf
andreamwolf.com

Angie Johnson
iheartnorwegianwood.etsy.com

Anja Hanschmann
spoonflower.com/profiles/annosch

Annabelle Ozanne
threeredapples.com

Anoushka Alden
byanoushka.etsy.com

Ayako mato Uemura
amujpn.etsy.com

Brianna Venner
thehappycouple.etsy.com

Carolyn Elliott
flickr.com/photos/geologyurbanfossil

Cheryl Warrick
www.warrickdesign.com

Chomp
chompindustries.com

Cloud 9 Fabrics
cloud9fabrics.com

Cynthia K. Strickland
studio80.etsy.com

Deborah O'Hare
quiltroutes.co.uk

Egle Minkuviene
jeweljazz.lt

Elena Klimora
flickr.com/busotherapy

Emilia Priscila
chicdecorpillows.etsy.com

Emily LeBaron
emskyrooney.blogspot.com

Erin Flett
erinflett.com

Estella Straatsma
starbags.etsy.com

Eva Reisinger
lakattun.de

Fabienne Chabrolin
flickr.com/people/reglissemint/

Heleen Webb
rubyinthedustdolls.blogspot.com

Hollabee
hollabee.blogspot.com

Holli Zollinger
hollizollinger.com

Jane Johnson, Tux and Tulle
tuxandtulle.etsy.com

Jennifer Ladd
jenniferladd.etsy.com

Jen Storey
jen.theypf.com

Jim Keaton
gardnerkeaton.com

Jo James and Dylan Curry
thecartbeforethehorse.com

Joshua By Oak
joshuabyoak.etsy.com

Julie Paschkis
juliepaschkis.com

Karen Lideen
thebeadedpillow.etsy.com

Karen Turner
stitchinglife.com

Kate Crossley
flickr.com/people/katecrossley

Keyka Lou
keykaloupatterns.com

Kirsti Michelle of Makenzi &
Madilyn Designs
im2keys.etsy.com

Kirsty Neale
kirstyneale.typepad.com

Laurie Dorrell
moonwild.blogspot.com

Leah Adams
kneek.etsy.com

Lori Kishlar and Sarah Melancon
thirdhalfstudios.com

Lori Sandstedt
lorimarsha.com

Lorie McCown
loriemccown.com

Lydia Meiying
hellomeiying.com

Lynn Harris
thelittleredhen.typepad.com

Marchi Wierson
marchiwierson.blogspot.com

Maria Rosa Lacerda Lage
mrosa-11@hotmail.com

IMAGE CREDITS

Mimi Oeberg
mymimi.com

Oksancia–Oksana Pasishnychenko
oksancia.com

Patty Sloniger
beckandlundy.blogspot.com

Rachel Winter
sweetpeaandco.etsy.com

Robin Romain
rawbonestudio.etsy.com

Sarah Walton
flickr.com/sarahwaltonembroidery

Sarah Waterhouse
sarahwaterhouse.co.uk

Sass & Peril
sassandperil.com

Shannon Benavidez of
Mayabella Creations
spoonflower.com/profiles/mayabella

Stella Padão
stellapadao@yahoo.com.br

Sue Reno
suereno.com

Susan Fitzgerald
spinspin.com

Suzanne Harlow
skybluesea.co.uk

Takuyo Williams
silkcouturebytakuyo.etsy.com

Tara Stewart
modernality2.etsy.com

Tuija Lommi
tuuni.etsy.com

Victoria Gertenbach
thesillyboodilly.blogspot.com

Whitlock & Co.
whitlockandco.etsy.com

Zesti–Ine Beerten
zesti.be

Cover and Introduction, Page 7:
Photography by Ryann Ford
ryannford.com
Photo styling by Robin Finlay

Introduction, Page 6:
Photography by Lisa Woods
nowandthenphotography.com

Ch 3:
Printing tutorials photographed by Umbrella Prints
Cyanotype tutorials photographed by Christina McFall

Ch 4:
Tutorials photographed by Frank McMains
frankmcmains.com

Ch 5:
Tutorials on pages 94–97, 102–105, and 110–113
photographed by Megan Van Sipe
Tutorials on pages 98–101 and 106–109
sewn by Brighton Sewing Centre
brightonsewingcentre.co.uk
Photographed by Ivan Jones
ivan-jones.co.uk

Ch 6:
Tutorials photographed by Lauren Volness Photography
Images on pages 124–127 reproduced courtesy of
Sublime Stitching

Ch 7:
Photography on pages 152–157 by Tara Badcock unless
otherwise credited

ABOUT THE AUTHOR

Laurie Wisbrun is a surface and textile designer based in Austin, Texas. She is the author of the blog *Scarlet Fig* and the book *Mastering the Art of Fabric Printing and Design*. She has a twenty-year background in marketing and is self-trained as a designer. She began designing fabric when she jumped off the corporate hamster wheel and was searching for a career where she could create designs that would surprise and delight retailers and consumers. Her aesthetic is about finding beauty in ordinary objects and patterns and playfully transforming them into stylish and modern designs with unexpected content and color combinations. Laurie has designed a number of international fabric collections, has licensed her designs to a number of home décor and stationery manufacturers, and sells limited-run fabric via her online Etsy store.

lauriewisbrun.com

Photo By Lisa Woods
www.nowandthenphotography.com